Cities of Art
in
Venice, Florence
and Rome

REG BUTLER

In Association with

CITYBREAKS
Thomson

SETTLE PRESS (WIGMORE)
HIPPOCRENE BOOKS INC.

While every reasonable care has been taken by the author and publisher in presenting the information in this book, no responsibility can be taken by them or by Thomson Holidays for any inaccuracies. Information and prices were correct at time of printing.
1989 Edition

Texts and maps © 1989 Reg Butler
All rights reserved. No part of this publication may be reproduced or transmitted in any form or by any means without permission.
First published by Settle Press (Wigmore)
32 Savile Row
London W1X 1AG

ISBN (Paperback) 0 907070 51 5

Published in United States by
Hippocrene Books Inc
171 Madison Avenue, New York
ISBN 0-87052-734-7

Printed by Villiers Publications Ltd
26a Shepherds Hill, London N6 5AH
Covers by Thumb Design Partnership
Maps by courtesy of the Italian State Tourist Office

Foreword

As Britain's leading short breaks specialist, we clearly recognise the need for detailed information and guidance for you, the would-be traveller. Yet a Citybreak is about more than museum opening times and table d'hôte tariffs, it's a quite sudden and easy submersion in the continental lifestyle – albeit for only a few days.

We were therefore particularly delighted to be able to work with Reg Butler and Settle Press on the City Breaks series. Reg Butler has provided for us a very readable book packed not only with important practical information but with colourful observations in a personal style that captures the very essence of your City Break city.

As well as City Breaks in Rome, Florence and Venice, you will find on the bookshelves City Breaks in Paris, Amsterdam, Moscow and Leningrad, and of course Thomson operate to 18 cities in Europe and the Americas from departure points across the UK.

We're sure you'll find this book invaluable in planning your short break in Venice, Florence and Rome.

THOMSON CITYBREAKS

Contents

		Page
1.	**INTRODUCTION TO CITY BREAKS**	
	1.1 On the grand Italian circuit	5
	1.2 Eating Out	7
	1.3 Your city break hotel	12
	1.4 At your service in Italy	13
2.	**VENICE, THE GONDOLA CITY**	
	2.1 Introduction	17
	2.2 Getting around	19
	2.3 Basic Venice	25
	2.4 Other sights	28
	2.5 Shopping	33
	2.6 Eating Out	35
	2.7 Nightlife	38
	2.8 Sunday in Venice	39
	2.9 At your service	40
3.	**FLORENCE**	
	3.1 Introduction	43
	3.2 Getting around	48
	3.3 Basic Florence	49
	3.4 Other sights	54
	3.5 Take a trip	60
	3.6 Shopping	62
	3.7 Eating Out	63
	3.8 Nightlife	67
	3.9 Sunday in Florence	68
	3.10 At your service	69
4.	**ROME**	
	4.1 Introduction	71
	4.2 Getting around	76
	4.3 Basic Rome	78
	4.4 Other sights	84
	4.5 Take a trip	93
	4.6 Shopping	94
	4.7 Eating Out	96
	4.8 Nightlife	100
	4.9 Sunday in Rome	102
	4.10 At your service	102

City Maps

Venice	20–23
Florence	44–47
Rome	72–75

Chapter One

Introduction to City Breaks

1.1 On the Grand Italian Circuit

No other nation can match so many touristic trump cards: Venice, Florence, Rome, Naples, Siena, Pisa . . . These Italian cities were focal-points of the old-style Grand Tour, which formerly was an essential part of a wealthy young man's education.

A rich man's son would develop a taste for paintings, sculpture and architecture; pick up some basic languages; learn something of history, and visit early Christian monuments; cultivate an ear for good music, and a taste for something more than English roast beef.

There was ample light relief on the Grand Tour: the pleasure of conversation with other grand travellers; going to masked balls and carnivals; flirting with the local girls; drinking the wines.

Today, few people can afford a year or two for an Italian Grand Tour. But the ease of modern air travel has brought the individual towns within easy reach of a long weekend city break. In 3 or 4 days, the 20th-century traveller can skim the sightseeing cream of a great city – look at the greatest masterpieces of painting and sculpture, explore classical remains, visit historic palaces.

On a one-week trip, there's ample scope for more in-depth cultivation of a particular interest, or for exploring other towns and the surrounding countryside on day excursions; or for combining cities in a two-centre arrangement.

The towns are *not* mere museum-pieces. Rome, Florence and Venice make up the super trio of Italy's highlight cities. Each has a totally different appeal. But they all offer the added bonus of an enviable way of life, a year-round mild climate, good eating with excellent low-priced wine, the pleasure of shop-gazing and wide choice of nightlife.

Rome has enough sightseeing to keep you busy for weeks: ancient ruins, miles of colossal city walls, catacombs and churches, monuments and fountains around every corner. Yet, amid this setting of dramatic remains from the past, the modern Roman exults in the 20th century.

There is no looking backwards, for instance, in the

postwar architecture of Rome. As you drive into town from the airport, your first view of Rome is ultra-modern: pastel-coloured apartments on the city outskirts.

Likewise in central Rome, look at the postwar Termini Railway Station, with its dramatically cantilevered roof that makes one gasp with its daring and imagination.

Yet away to one side, left untouched as an integral part of the architect's plan, is a large selection of original Roman wall, built 2000 years ago. That sight is symbolic. It reminds us that the Rome of today mixes quite well with the Rome of ancient history.

Going round central Rome is like travelling on a Time Machine. There are columns which stood there when Julius Caesar was just back from conquering Britain; the jail where St Peter was locked up; the tower of a medieval palace, a facade by Michelangelo, or a church by Bernini; the balcony from which Mussolini declared war on Britain.

As the capital of the Catholic world, the Vatican City is a place of pilgrimage to millions every year. Even to non-Catholics, there is great sense of awe on those occasions when the Pope emerges at midday onto his balcony, and pronounces a blessing on all the thousands gathered below in St Peter's Square. And you think of all the pilgrim millions who have likewise been blessed over the centuries . . .

A visit to Rome is a journey into the past, greatly enlivened by the present. That's equally true of Florence and Venice.

Florence is an art-lovers' paradise, with some of the world's richest collections of Renaissance paintings and sculpture. But its full appeal is not buried in museums. Few other cities have such magnificent antique stores, alternating with workshops of a dozen different living crafts: leather and raffia work, gold and silver jewellery, art reproductions, mosaics and exquisite embroidery. Florence can rank as the top rival to Paris for high fashion, glittering with great names but still leaving room for hundreds of small boutiques to make a decent living.

Step carelessly off the pavement in Rome or Florence, and you risk being mown down by passing traffic. It's quite different in Venice, where you can gossip in the middle of the street, just like a thousand years ago when the original paving stones were laid. Venice is full of exuberant activity such as carnival time in early February when the 18th century is revived with masked balls and pageants. Visitors flock through the central piazza – behind their guide-lecturers in the morning, free in the afternoon. Night-time, the canals echo to the sound of Gondola Serenades.

When's the best season for an Italian city break?

Rome, Florence and Venice are cities for all seasons. Springtime, especially at Easter, the big rush starts. In the hotter summer months, many sightseers adopt the good Italian tradition of an afternoon siesta. It's not a 'waste' of time. They are then refreshed for a cooler return to the sightseeing circuits, followed by the tranquil pleasures of open-air dining, watching the world go by from pavement cafés or attending open-air opera.

Autumn is well worth considering, for easier progress around the tourist sites. Finally, let's remember that, during the days of the Grand Tour, the illustrious travellers of the 18th and 19th centuries regularly wintered in Rome. December onwards, the musical and social scene is in full swing, offering quite a different picture from the Rome of high summer season.

So any long weekend can be a good time to visit Italy. Out-of-pocket expenses are quite reasonable. At least a hundred valid reasons exist for a civilised human being to sample the cultural and scenic riches that Italy can offer. Quite apart from the cultural scene, the Italian cities are places to enjoy yourself and have fun.

Of course, it's impossible to absorb more than a tiny fraction of Italy's potential in a single trip. The only solution is to limit yourself to one or two of the great cities, and leave the rest till 'next time'.

1.2 Eating Out in Italy

If you go overboard for Italian cuisine with Italian wine, you can have glorious eating at reasonable cost, with enormous choice of restaurants. It's much more fun than eating standard 'international' menus in the tourist hotels. Don't worry if you cannot speak Italian – just wave and point. But most waiters have basic English.

Italy features three main kinds of restaurant – 'osteria', 'trattoria' and 'ristorante', in ascending order of quality and price, though nowadays the distinction is blurring.

If you cannot manage a full meal at lunch-time, there are plenty of chances for snacks. Many bars have a selection of sandwiches called 'tramezzini' which have very appetising fillings.

There's another type of restaurant/café called 'tavola calda', where you can get simple hot dishes at reasonable price. They are dotted all over Italy's principal cities. Customers eat standing up – dishes of spaghetti, ravioli or whatever the dish of the day happens to be. It's very handy for a quick lunch, if you don't want a full sit-down meal spread over a couple of hours.

At a pizzeria, you can fill up with a bowl of thick minestrone and a huge pizza that overlaps a dinner plate.

For picnic eating, there is good, cheap fruit – oranges, cherries, melons, peaches, apricots, grapes, fresh figs, according to season. Excellent cheeses, cooked meats and salads help keep outgoings low.

Learn the Italian word *etto*, which means hectogramme

or 100 grammes. For quick guidance, reckon it's a quarter-pound or four ounces. Fish or steak dishes are frequently priced per *etto*, not per portion. Know the system, and save yourself a nasty shock when the bill comes.

There is something very typically Italian about the snack bars dominated by a massive Espresso machine, gleaming and polished and steaming. On the shelves behind are bottles of every conceivable spirit and liqueur known to European man. These establishments are also useful as a stopping-point for a quick sandwich. At a typical cafeteria, black coffee costs 700 lire; cappuccino, 900 lire.

In the mornings from 7 to 11 a.m. you'll find Italians having their breakfasts of capuccinos and cornettos (croissants). However, if you feel in need of a brandy or a martini, you will not be on your own!

If you take a drink at the bar, you must normally pay first at the cash desk (cassa). Take the receipt to the bar, put a 100 lire coin on top of it (watch the Romans here), and tell the barman what you want. The tip ensures rapid service. Standing at the bar is always much cheaper than having drinks and sandwiches served to a table. You're not supposed to buck the system by ordering at the bar, and then sitting down.

A standard 'menu turistico' comprises a flat-rate 3-course menu, usually with a drink such as beer or quarter-litre of wine, service and tax. The price may be reasonable enough, but don't expect any gastronomic delights.

All restaurants charge 'coperto', which is a per-person cover charge. Then there is a service charge 'servizio' which can be from 10–20% on the total bill. Tipping is not necessary on top, unless for exceptional service. VAT is added. Keep your restaurant bill, as tax inspectors are making valiant attempts to keep tabs on the catering trade. Within 200 metres of a restaurant, inspectors can ask you to produce your receipt: otherwise, a hefty fine. For the tourist, it's all rather theoretical.

Plenty of Pasta

In Italy you can eat pasta twice a day during a one-week city break, and come nowhere near repeating yourself. The variations on the pasta theme are enormous. It comes mainly in two colours: the usual cream colour; and green, made by working spinach into the paste. It's also made in a huge variety of shapes. Lifetime students of pasta break down mamma's favourite food into five main categories:

1. Rope or string, e.g. Spaghetti
2. Ribbon, e.g. Tagliatelle
3. Tubes, e.g. Penne
4. Envelopes, e.g. Ravioli
5. Fancy shapes like shells or wheels, e.g. Conchiglie, Tortellini.

Here's a short list to sample:

Agnolotti/Anolini	Small stuffed envelopes, like ravioli
Cannelloni	Large tubes, stuffed with various meat, and baked in cheese and tomato sauce
Cappellitti	Twists of pasta, usually stuffed and served in a light sauce. The Roman version of tortellini
Conchiglie	Shell-shaped pasta
Farfalloni	Pasta in the shape of a butterfly
Fettuccine	Thin ribbon pasta made with egg. The Roman name for tagliatelle
Fusilli	Skeins of ribbon pasta
Lasagne	Ribbon pasta, usually baked after boiling
Lasagne verdi	Green lasagne
Penne	Small tubes
Pastini	Small, fine pasta in a variety of shapes for soup
Ravioli	Small envelopes, stuffed with a meat, vegetable or cheese filling
Rigatoni	Large grooved tubes
Spaghetti	Need anything be said? But spaghetti can still be sub-divided into capellini, fusilli, spaghettini, spirale and vermicelli
Tagliatelle	Ribbon pasta about a quarter of an inch wide
Tortellini	Little twists of pasta with a rich stuffing and a variety of delicate sauces
Torteloni	Large coils of stuffed pasta

Guide to Menu Items

Zuppe e Antipasti	*Soups and Starters*
Gamberetti	Shrimps
Granchio	Crabs
Melone con fichi	Melon with figs
Melone con prosciutto	Melon with ham
Misto or frutti di mare	Mixed seafood
Panada	Broth
Zuppa di pesce	Fish soup
Zuppa di fagioli	Bean soup
Risotti e Pasta	*Rice and Pasta dishes*
Asparagi	Risotto with asparagus
Nere de seppie	Risotto with cuttlefish in its ink
Primavera	Risotto with diced fresh vegetables
Bigoli	Dark coloured pasta

Pasta e fagioli	Pasta with white bean soup
Risi e Anguilla	Rice and eel
Risi e bisi	Rice and peas

Pesce e Crostacei — *Fish and shellfish*

Anguilla	Eel
Aringa	Herring
Baccala	Cod
Branzino	Sea bass
Calamari	Squid
Cozze	Mussels
Frutta di mare	Seafood
Gamberelli	Prawns
Granchi	Shrimps
Nasello	Haddock
Ostriche	Oysters
Pesce spada	Swordfish
Salmone	Salmon
Sgombro	Mackerel
Sogliola	Plaice
Sogliola Finta	Sole
Tonno	Tuna
Triglia	Red Mullet
Trota	Trout

Carne — *Meat*

Agnello	Lamb
Anatra/anitra	Duck
Bistecca	Steak
Bistecca de Filetto	Fillet steak
Braciola	Cutlet, chop
Bue	Beef
Coniglio	Rabbit
Coscia	Leg
Cotoletta/Costata	Cutlet/chop
Fagiona	Pheasant
Faraona	Guinea Fowl
Fegato	Liver
Maiale	Pork
Manzo	Beef
Montone	Mutton
Pollo	Chicken
Prosciutto	Ham
Ragout	Stew
Rognoni	Kidneys
Rosbif	Roast beef
Salsicce	Sausage
Salsicce alla Griglia	Grilled sausage
Selvaggina	Venison
Tacchino	Turkey
Tournedo	Rump steak
Vitello	Veal

Verdura	*Vegetables*
Aglio	Garlic
Barbabietola/Bietola	Beetroot
Broccoli	Broccoli
Carciofi	Artichokes
Carotte	Carrots
Cavolfiore	Cauliflower
Cetriolo	Cucumber
Cipolle	Onions
Fagioli	Beans
Funghi	Mushrooms
Insalata	Salad
Lattuga	Lettuce
Melanzane	Aubergines
Patate	Potatoes
Peperoni	Peppers
Piselli	Peas
Pomodoro	Tomato
Spinaci	Spinach
Dolci	*Desserts*
Baicoli	Venetian cookies
Bussolai	Traditional biscuits from Burano
Gelato	Ice cream
Tirami su	Rich dessert soaked in coffee and liqueur, and covered in cream
Zabaglione	Dessert made with egg yolks and Marsala
Zuppa inglese	Trifle
Frutta	*Fruit*
Albicocca	Apricot
Ananas	Pineapple
Anguria	Water melon
Arancia	Orange
Ciliege	Cherries
Fragole	Strawberries
Frutta fresca	Fresh fruit
Lamponi	Raspberries
Mela	Apple
Pera	Pear
Pesca	Peach
Pompelmo	Grapefruit
Prugna	Plum
Bibite	*Drinks*
Acqua Minerale	Mineral water
Birra	Beer
Caffè	Black coffee
Cappucino	White coffee
Latte	Milk

Tè	Tea
Vino – rosso/bianco	Wine – red/white

Miscellaneous

Burro	Butter
Formaggio	Cheese
Frittata	Omelette
Gnocchi	Dumplings
Minestra	Soup
Pane	Bread
Salsa	Sauce
Uova	Eggs

Cooking terms

Arrosto	Roast
Crudo	Raw
Còtto	Cooked
Stufato	Stew

1.3 Your City Break Hotel

Check-in:

Normal check-in and check-out time is midday, but confirm with reception. If you arrive before noon, you may check in and leave luggage with reception until your room is free. If your final departure is after midday, pack bags before going out for the morning and leave them in the left-luggage room.

Getting in Late:

Some hotels lock their doors after midnight. If you plan to be out late, it's a good idea to advise the concierge beforehand, just to be sure that a night porter can let you in!

Electricity:

Italian electricity is 220 volts (though, exceptionally, a few hotels in Venice are on 110 V). Plugs are generally Continental-style two-pin. Pack a plug adaptor if you expect to use your own electric gadgets.

Lighting:

Hotel corridors sometimes have a time switch for the lights, long enough to unlock your door. Look for a small orange light and press the button.

Water taps:

'C' stands for *caldo*, meaning hot, 'F' is *freddo*, meaning cold.

Breakfast:

Italian breakfasts are Continental – bread or rolls, jam or

marmalade, with butter, and tea or coffee. Normally it's served early, available between 7.30 and 9.30.

Tipping:
Around 500 lire per case is usual for porters. Chambermaids will appreciate the lire you leave for them in the bedroom at the end of your stay.

1.4 At Your Service in Italy

Money & Banking

Currency:
The Italian unit of currency is the lira (plural lire).

Coins	Notes
100 lire	1,000 lire
200 lire	2,000 lire
500 lire	5,000 lire
	10,000 lire
	50,000 lire
	100,000 lire

The symbol used for marking prices is similar to the pound sterling sign – £.

Unless you're very fast at mental arithmetic, Italian lire are confusing for the first day or two. Suggestion: before departure, check the current exchange rate, and list out some conversions on a postcard, as a handy crib.

There is often a shortage of small change, and telephone tokens, sweets or stamps may be used to make up the deficiency.

Changing Money:
Take a starter kit of a bundle of lire, to tide you over the first day or two in Italy, especially if you arrive at weekends. You can change money and cheques at the arrival airport or railway terminus. Banks are normally open 8.30 a.m. till 1.20 p.m., and for a variable hour in the afternoon, Monday till Friday, closed weekends. Rates vary from bank to bank, so it's worth comparing their display panels. A flat commission charge of up to 3000 lire on Traveller Cheques makes it uneconomic to change little and often. Some Exchange Bureaux keep longer hours. Larger hotels can also oblige, but give unfriendly rates. Always take your passport with you.

Personal Cheques & Eurocheques:
Eurocheques, with the appropriate banker's card, are among the simplest and most acceptable means of payment.

These must be specially ordered from your bank, but are well worth it, as you can write the cheques in the local currency. They can also be used in UK. The Eurocheque card allows you to cash up to £100 per day, and is also valid to make payments to shops, hotels and restaurants that display the Eurocheque sign. Normal cheques backed by a banker's card up to £50 are also accepted in many places.

Credit Cards:

Access, Visa, American Express and Diners Club are widely accepted at shops and restaurants. At some banks you can withdraw cash, but it's often inconvenient: don't over-rely on credit cards for getting cash.

Reconverting Cash:

In general, convert any surplus lire back into sterling or dollars at the departure airport. Avoid taking 50,000 and 100,000 lire notes back into the UK, as banks may refuse to change them and certainly will give a lower rate.

Post Office & Telephone

Post Offices (Ufficio Postale) handle telegrams, mail and money transfers, and some have public telephones. Opening hours are generally Mon/Fri 8.15/14.00 hours. Stamps are also sold at tobacconists' (tabaccheria) with a 'T' sign above the door. They're a lot more helpful if you buy some postcards at the same time! Likewise, some hotel desks carry a stamp supply. Stamps are 'francobolli' in Italian.

Post boxes are red, and non-local mail should be posted in the slot marked 'altre destinazioni'.

Telephone Calls (International)

Making long distance and international calls from hotels is an expensive luxury! Instead, go to the nearest office of S.I.P. (pronounced 'seep') – standing for Società Italiana Posta/Telefoni. There's a line of cabins, and a queue. When your turn comes, the counter clerk will tell you which booth number to use.

(1) Dial 00 for International Exchange, and wait for a tone change.
(2) Dial 44 (the international code for UK) plus the appropriate STD town dialling code, minus the first zero; then the local number. Thus, to call Barnsley (code 0226) 12345, dial 0044 226 12345. Other country codes are: USA and Canada 1; Australia 61; New Zealand 64.
(3) Afterwards, you return to the desk to pay for the telephone call. Calls are cheaper after 22.00 hours, and at the weekend.

Coin Boxes:

For local calls, you'll need two 100-lire coins or one 200-lire coin for the modern call box; or a 'gettone' (token) which costs 200 lire at a bar. Lift receiver, dial, and insert the gettone when the connection is made. 'Guasto' means broken or out of order. Long distance calls can also be made from telephone boxes with a yellow disc and the word 'teleselezione' or 'interurbana'. *To call Italy* from other countries, the international code is 39. Thus, from Britain, dial 010-39- Italian area code less the first zero – the local number.

Medical

Should you require a doctor, contact your hotel concierge and ask him to call one.

If you have holiday or medical insurance, get receipts both from the doctor and the chemist, so as to make any necessary reclaim. If you're on a package tour, and sizeable funds are needed to cover medical expenses, contact your tour operator Representative for advice.

As part of EEC reciprocal health arrangements, UK visitors can get all dental and medical services that are available to Italians. Before departure from Britain, ask your local Department of Health and Social Security (DHSS) office for 'Medical Costs Abroad' leaflet no. SA30. Fill out the form CM1 and send it to the DHSS, who will supply form E111 to take with you. It's probably not worth the effort for minor ailments, but would be most useful if anything major happened.

Chemists are open only during normal shop hours, but a window sign indicates the nearest night or Sunday-opening chemist ('farmacia').

Pickpockets

Just like in any other European country, hardworking pickpockets specialise in the tourist traffic. Their guess is that holidaymaker handbags or wallets will contain an above-average supply of currency, traveller cheques and credit cards. International teams are also at work during the season, often looking just like other tourists.

Be particularly careful in crowded places, especially if travelling by bus. Pickpockets frequently work in pairs, taking advantage of crowds to jostle or distract their victims while stealing a purse or wallet. In narrow side-streets, skilled riders on scooters have perfected a motorised bag-snatching technique as they swoop past.

There's no need to go overboard with suspicion of all strangers. But it's sensible not to make things easy for crooks. **Keep handbags fastened and held securely, preferably under your arm. Never carry a wallet in your hip pocket.**

Minimise any potential loss by leaving the bulk of your valuables in the safety deposits available to hotel guests. Keep a separate record of traveller-cheque numbers, and also of credit-card details of where to notify in case of loss.

If you have anything stolen, report the theft to the nearest police station and obtain an official declaration of theft, required for insurance reclaim. If you're on a package tour with insurance cover, contact the tour operator Representative for advice on making a 'Loss Report' to send with your claim form.

Female Harrassment

Of course, it does exist. Best advice is to ignore the persistent overtures, until the young idiots get tired of the game and try elsewhere. Otherwise, say 'NO!' in loud English. It means the same in Italian.

Climate

TEMPERATURES – midday averages (°F)

	Jan	Feb	Mar	Apr	May	Jun	Jul	Aug	Sep	Oct	Nov	Dec
Venice	42	46	53	62	70	77	81	80	75	65	53	46
Florence	48	52	58	66	74	80	86	85	78	69	57	51
Rome	52	55	59	66	76	82	86	86	79	71	61	55

RAINFALL – monthly averages (inches)

	Jan	Feb	Mar	Apr	May	Jun	Jul	Aug	Sep	Oct	Nov	Dec
Venice	2.3	1.5	2.9	3.0	2.8	2.8	1.5	1.9	2.8	2.6	3.0	2.1
Florence	2.4	2.7	2.5	2.9	2.4	1.9	0.9	1.5	2.1	2.8	4.2	2.8
Rome	2.9	3.4	3.1	2.4	2.2	1.5	0.2	0.9	2.6	4.8	4.8	3.6

SEA TEMPERATURE – average (°F)

	Apr	May	Jun	Jul	Aug	Sep	Oct
Venice Lido	59	63	79	81	79	72	64

Public Holidays

1 January	New Year's Day
6 January	Epiphany
25 April	Liberation Day, 1945
Easter Monday	
1 May	May Day
Ascension	
Corpus Christi	
2 June	Proclamation of the Republic
15 August	Assumption
1 November	All Saints
4 November	National Unity Day
8 December	Immaculate Conception
25 & 26 December	Christmas

Chapter Two

Venice – The Gondola City

2.1 Introduction

Part of the fun of Venice is seeing first-hand how a city can work without wheels.

There's real theatre about your arrival: travelling by road or rail by causeway across the Venetian lagoon, and then finding water transport – bus, taxi or gondola – to your hotel.

Main Street is the Grand Canal: 2 miles long, 80 yards wide, and shaped like the backward 'S' of a simple speller. All is magnificence. The finest palaces, churches, museums and mansions line its banks. Every bend offers a vista that seems almost too highly-coloured to be true.

The essential monuments – Cathedral, Clock Tower, Campanile, Doges' Palace – stand side by side on St Mark's Square, where rival open-air café orchestras play for their clientele and the passers-by.

That's an entertainment in itself, just sitting for an hour, drinking a beer and idly watching the world-wide cross-section of tourists and pretty girls. You pay a high price for the setting – for the privilege of enjoying your refreshment in one of Europe's most beautiful squares, virtually unchanged since the 16th century. But few visitors complain at the bill, when the location is so perfect.

Go just around the corner to a side-canal bar, and a similar beer will cost barely one-third the price.

There's great enjoyment in venturing through medieval alleys into little piazzas, walking beside canals and over the hump-backed bridges. Everywhere you point your camera, there are pictures. Just drift around at random, away from the main stream of tourism, and you'll find new delight at every corner.

Take a carefree attitude towards time, and getting lost for an hour doesn't matter. Distances are really quite small, like in Hampton Court Maze. An expert navigator can walk right across Venice in 30 minutes. The less expert could make out in two or three hours, but would carry away a lifetime's memory of a journey through the Middle Ages. That's the Venetian experience.

The full enjoyment of Venice depends how you approach

it. Read up some potted history – the incredible story of how a group of muddy islands became the greatest art and trading centre of medieval Europe – and the Venice of today will really come alive.

It all started in 5th century AD, when the Roman Empire was falling apart and Barbarians were sweeping down the middle of Italy. A few refugees from mainland cities settled in these islands, protected by waters of the Lagoon. They stayed independent, and elected their first *dux* or Doge in year 726.

Over the centuries, the Venetians became shrewd traders and businessmen, linking the trading routes from Asia Minor to northern Europe. Commanding the main route to the Holy Land, they particularly made big profits from the Crusades – cash down, and a share of the loot for providing army transport ships. As part of the contracts, the Venetians acquired trading rights in many Levant cities, and supremacy in the Adriatic.

Their biggest pay-off came from the Crusader sacking of Constantinople in 1204. Quite apart from their share of Byzantine treasures, the Venetians gained control of all strategic locations and trading posts in Eastern Mediterranean and through to the Black Sea. Venice commanded the Silk Route to the Far East, and had a virtual monopoly of the overland spice trade from the Indies.

Thanks to that commercial supremacy, the merchants and ruling families of Venice became extremely wealthy. They lined the Grand Canal with rich palaces and public buildings, furnished with great luxury. Artists and craftsmen flocked to the city, where big money flowed.

Later, the power of Venice dwindled. The Turks captured Constantinople in 1453. With expansion of the Ottoman Empire, the Venetians lost most of their maritime possessions. A major blow to their commercial supremacy came in 1486, when Vasco da Gama opened up a new round-the-Cape sea route for the spice trade. With discovery of the Americas, Venice was on the 'wrong' side of the Mediterranean to exploit the business potential. In early 16th century, many of Venetian territories were carved up by an alliance called the League of Cambrai, comprising the European powers, the Church, and other Italian States.

But, despite the trading decline and loss of empire, Venice still flourished as the aristocratic fun city of Europe, full of courtesans, festivals, masked balls, high-stake gambling, pleasure of every kind. Venice was an essential staging-point on a wealthy young man's Grand Tour, whence he could return to his country estate with souvenir sculptures and paintings. All the great Italian painters – Giorgione, Titian, Tintoretto, Veronese, and then Canaletto and many others – found a rich clientele for their work, and dozens of churches to decorate.

The good days continued until the French Revolution,

followed by decades of melancholy and neglect. For the past hundred-odd years, international tourism has kept Venice alive – just as international aid funds are helping to prevent Venice sinking permanently into the mud. The festival tradition continues, and Venice keeps its repute as one of the great fun cities of Europe. It's a wonderful place to enjoy yourself, with masses of culture as an excuse for going, if you need an excuse.

2.2 Getting Around in Venice

After the first few hours, you'll start getting your bearings. Studying the map, check how your hotel relates to the main points of Venice. Most important is the Grand Canal, running in backward-S shape from Railway Station and Piazzale Roma at the north end, through to St Mark's at the south.

There are only three bridges across Grand Canal: Scalzi – north; Rialto – central; Accademia – south. From Piazzale Roma to Accademia and St Mark's, an important short-cut canal called Rio Nuovo avoids the big upper swing of the Grand Canal.

The public transport system is wrapped around the points on these waterways. The Venetian water buses – 'Vaporetti' – are almost as famous as the gondolas, but not nearly so romantic. Especially beware of pickpockets.

Tickets are sold at the entrance to each water bus stand. Anyone caught aboard without a valid ticket risks an on-the-spot fine. But you can also buy tickets on board, at a 500-lire supplement. Standard single fares are 1,500 lire, except for the Fast Vaporetto No. 2 – the 'Diretto' – which is 2,000 lire.

A tourist ticket ('Biglietto Turistico') costs 8,000 lire and is valid for 24 hours on any line. For a couple on a city break, it's worth buying a book of ten tickets, costing 15,000 lire. This will save you having to queue each time. A ticket must be cancelled in the machine before entering the landing stage area.

Vaporetti Routes

The water buses run every ten minutes or so during the day, and less frequently between midnight and 7 a.m.

There are 20 bus stops on the main Canal Grande to Lido route:

1 – Piazzale Roma; 2 – Ferrovia (railway station); 3 – Riva di Biagio; 4 – San Marcuola; 5 – San Staè; 6 – Ca' d'Oro; 7 – Rialto; 8 – San Silvestro; 9 – San Angelo; 10 – San Tomà (Frari Church); 11 – Ca' Rezzonico; 12 – Accademia; 13 – Santa Maria del Giglio (Fenice); 14 – Salute; 15 – San Marco; 16 – San Zaccaria; 17 – Arsenale; 18 – Giardini (Esposizione); 19 – Santa Elena; 20 – Lido.

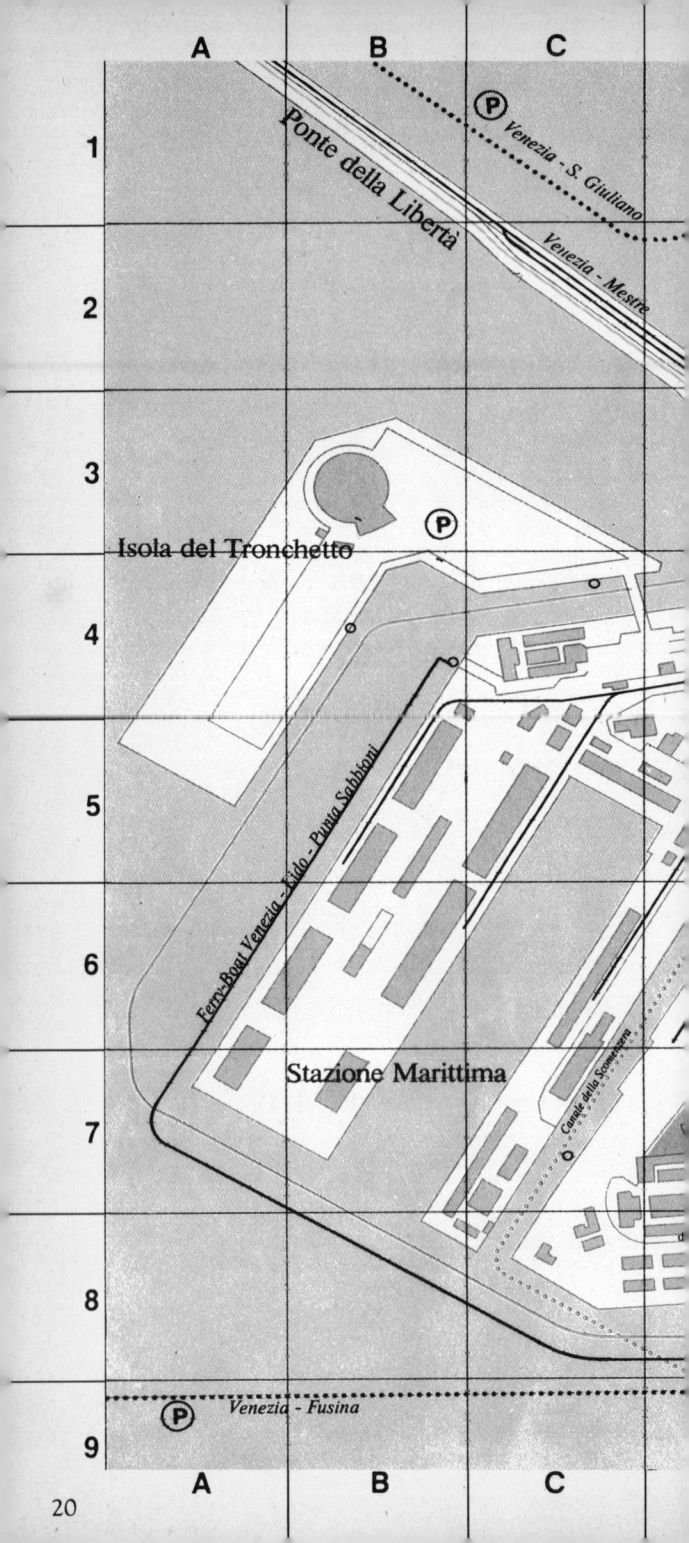

	A	B	C
1		Ponte della Libertà	Ⓟ Venezia - S. Giuliano
2			Venezia - Mestre
3			Ⓟ
4	Isola del Tronchetto		
5		Ferry-Boat Venezia - Lido - Punta Sabbioni	
6			
7		Stazione Marittima	Canale della Scomenzera
8			
9	Ⓟ	Venezia - Fusina	

21

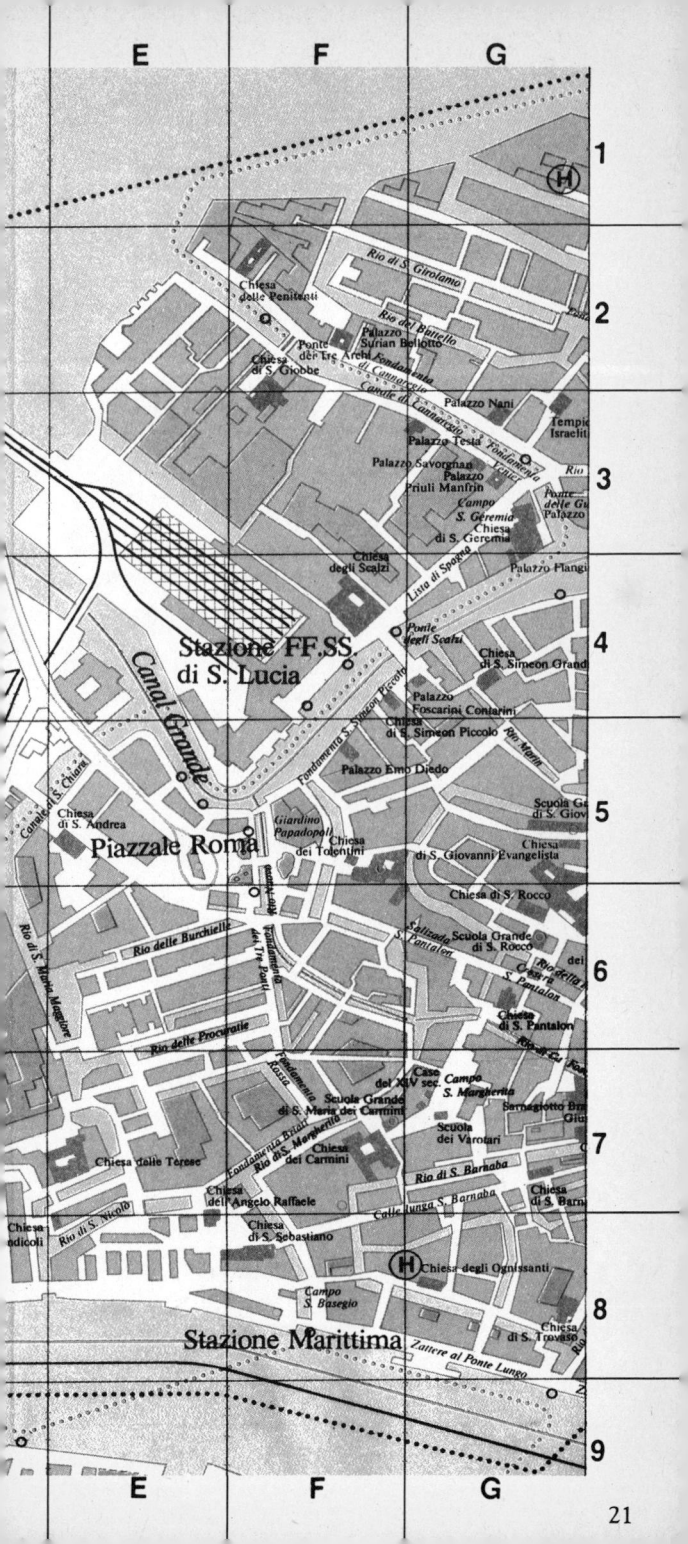

H
I
J
1
2
3
4
5
6
7
8
9
Rio di S. Alvise
Chiesa di S. Alvise
Chiesa della Madonna dell'Orto
Fondamenta della Sensa
Rio della Madonna dell'Orto
Campo dei Mori
Rio della Sensa
Fondamenta degli Ormesini
Calle della Malvasia
Campo del Ghetto
Palazzo Mastelli o del Cammello
Rio della Misericordia
Fondamenta della Misericordia
Chiesa dei Servi
Fondamenta dell'Abbazia
Chiesa della Misericordia
Scuola Vecchia della Misericordia
Rio di S. Fosca
Palazzo Diedo
Rio Terrà di S. Leonardo
Chiesa di S. Marcuola
Palazzo Vendramin Calergi
Chiesa della Maddalena
Scuola Grande di S. Maria della Misericordia
Chiesa di S. Caterina
Palazzo Correr Contarini
Palazzo Erizzo
Palazzo Soranzo Piovene
Chiesa di S. Fosca
Rio di Noale
Rio di S. Felice
Palazzo Giovanelli Dorigo
Fondaco dei Turchi
Deposito del Megio
Palazzo Belloni Battagia
Palazzo Gussoni
Chiesa di S. Felice
Palazzo Fontana Rezzonico
Palazzo Priuli Bon
Ca' Tron
Canal Grande
Chiesa di S. Zan Degolà
Rio di San Zan Degolà
Chiesa di S. Sofia
Strada Nova
Palazzo Giusti
Ca' D'Oro
Ca' Pesaro
Chiesa di S. Stae
Chiesa dei SS. Apostoli
Ca' Sagredo
Palazzo Corner della Regina
Chiesa di S. Maria Mater Domini
Chiesa di S. Giacomo dell'Orio
Palazzo Michiel delle Colonne
Campo SS. Apostoli
Palazzo Mangilli Valmarana
Palazzo Brandolin già dei Morosini
Ca' da Mosto
Campo S. Giacomo dell'Orio
Fabbriche Nuove e Vecchie
Case del XIII sec.
Chiesa di S. Cassiano
Palazzo Civran
Chiesa di S. Giacometto
Palazzo dei Camerlenghi
Chiesa di S. Giovanni Elemosinario
Fontego dei Tedeschi
Palazzo Corner Mocenigo
Palazzi Soranzo
Palazzo dei Dieci Savi
Rio di S. Polo
Campo S. Polo
Chiesa di S. Aponal
Chiesa di S. Silvestro
Ponte di Rialto
Campo S. Bortolomio
Chiesa di S. Bortolomio
Chiesa dei Frari
Chiesa di S. Polo
Ca' Barzizza
Palazzo Businello
Palazzo Dolfin Manin
Campo dei Frari
Palazzo Donà della Madonetta
Palazzo Papadopoli
Palazzo Bembo
Palazzo Donà
Scuola Grande di S. Teodoro
Chiesa di S. Salvador
Merceria
Scuola Calegheri
Casa dei Goldoni
Ca' Loredan
Palazzo Bernardo
Palazzo Grimani
Ca' Farsetti
Palazzo Grimani
Campo S. Tomà
Palazzo Pisani
Palazzo Persico
Palazzo Martinengo Volpi
Palazzo Corner Contarini dei Cavalli
Campo S. Luca
Chiesa di S. Luca
Calle dei Fabbri
Campo Manin
Palazzo Corner Spinelli
Palazzo Fortuny
Palazzo Civran Grimani
Palazzi Mocenigo
Calle della Mandola
Rio di S. Luca
Palazzo Balbi
Palazzo Contarini delle Figure
Procuratie Vecchie
Ca' Foscari
Palazzo Erizzo Nani Mocenigo
Palazzo Moro Lin
Campo S. Angelo
Palazzo Duodo
Chiesa di S. Fantin
Palazzo Grassi
Chiesa di S. Samuele
Scuola Grande di S. Fantin
Chiesa di S. Stefano
Chiesa di S. Moisè
Ca' Rezzonico
Palazzo Malipiero
Campo S. Stefano
Teatro La Fenice
Calle Larga XXII Marzo
Palazzo Loredan
Palazzo Giustinian Lolin
Rio di S. Moisè
Chiesa di S. Vidal
Palazzo Pisani
Chiesa di S. Maria del Giglio
Ca' Giustinian
Palazzo Contarini degli Scrigni
Palazzo Franchetti Cavalli
Palazzo Venier Contarini
Palazzo Contarini Fasan
Palazzo Flangini Fini
Scuola Grande di S. Maria della Carità
Ponte dell'Accademia
Ca' Corner
Palazzo Contarini del Zaffo
Abbazia di S. Gregorio
Chiesa della Salute
Gallerie dell'Accademia
Palazzo da Mula
Palazzo Dario
Dogana
Rio Terrà Foscarini
Campo S. Vio
Rio di S. Trovaso
Chiesa di S. Maria della Visitazione
Chiesa dei Gesuati
Palazzo Venier dei Leoni
Palazzo Barbaro
Chiesa di S. Gregorio
Rio di S. Vio
Rio della Fornace
Chiesa di S. Agnese
Chiesa dello Spirito Santo
Zattere ai Gesuati
Zattere allo Spirito Santo
Zattere ai Saloni

Venice map (grid L–N, rows 1–9)

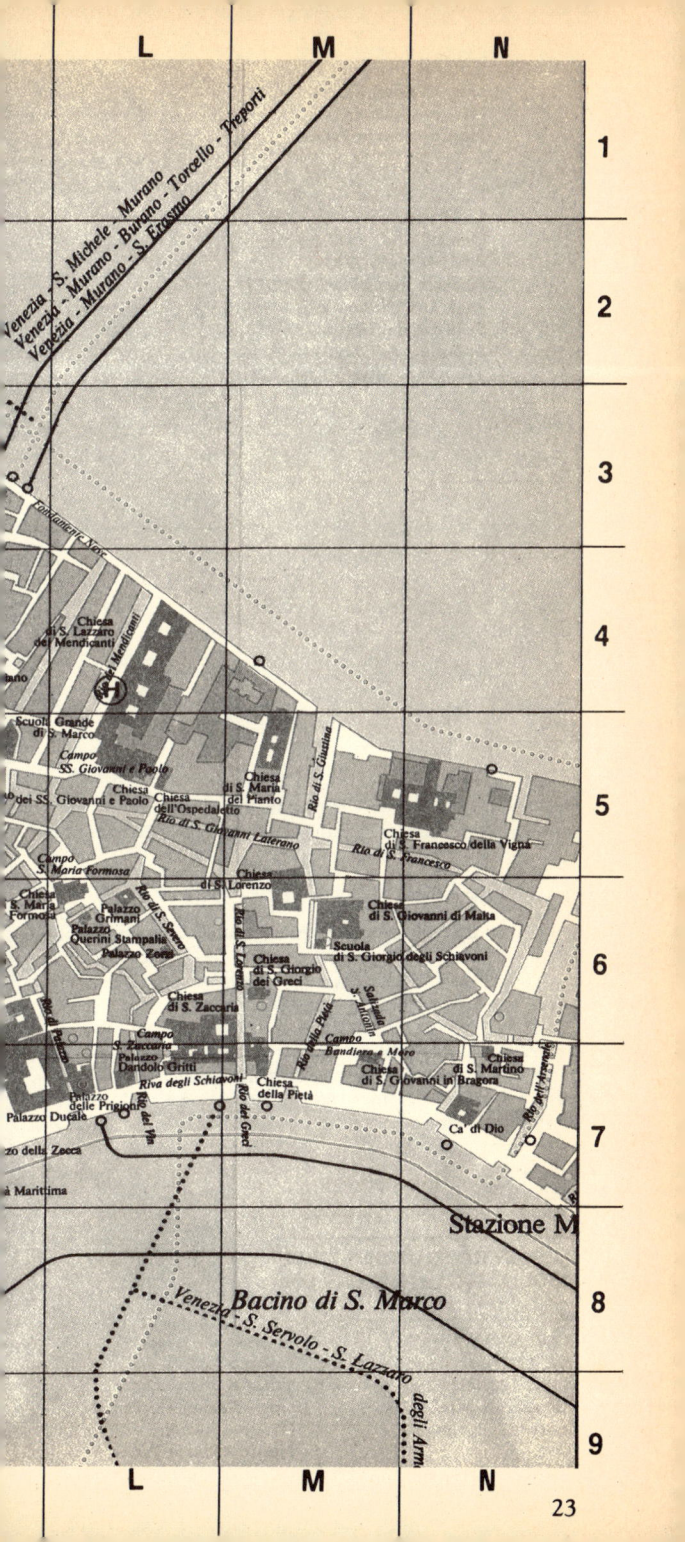

Ferry routes (upper left):
- Venezia – S. Michele – Murano – Burano – Torcello – Treporti
- Venezia – Murano – Burano – S. Erasmo
- Venezia – Murano – S. Erasmo

Fondamenta Nove

Row 4–5 (left side):
- Chiesa di S. Lazzaro dei Mendicanti
- Scuola Grande di S. Marco
- Campo SS. Giovanni e Paolo
- Chiesa dei SS. Giovanni e Paolo
- Chiesa dell'Ospedaletto
- Chiesa di S. Maria del Pianto
- Rio di S. Giovanni Laterano
- Rio di S. Giustina
- Chiesa di S. Francesco della Vigna
- Rio di S. Francesco

Row 6:
- Campo S. Maria Formosa
- Chiesa S. Maria Formosa
- Palazzo Grimani
- Palazzo Querini Stampalia
- Palazzo Zorzi
- Rio di Palazzo
- Rio di S. Severo
- Rio di S. Lorenzo
- Chiesa di S. Lorenzo
- Chiesa di S. Giorgio dei Greci
- Chiesa di S. Zaccaria
- Chiesa di S. Giovanni di Malta
- Scuola di S. Giorgio degli Schiavoni
- Salizada S. Antonin

Row 7:
- Campo S. Zaccaria
- Palazzo Dandolo Gritti
- Palazzo delle Prigioni
- Palazzo Ducale
- Palazzo della Zecca
- Riva degli Schiavoni
- Rio del Vin
- Rio dei Greci
- Chiesa della Pietà
- Campo Bandiera e Moro
- Chiesa di S. Giovanni in Bragora
- Chiesa di S. Martino
- Ca' di Dio
- Rio dell'Arsenale

Stazione M(arittima)

Row 8: Bacino di S. Marco

Venezia – S. Servolo – S. Lazzaro degli Arm(eni)

Route 1 – Accelerato
Calls at every stop from 1 to 20. Stops 1 to 15 (San Marco) cover the entire length of Grand Canal. Journey time, right through to Lido – one hour; or about 45 minutes to San Marco.

Route 2 – Diretto
Express service with fewer stops, from Rialto Bridge (stop 7) to the Lido di Venezia, via Ferrovia and Piazzale Roma (stops 2 and 1), and then takes the short cut through Rio Nuovo to St Mark's and the Lido.

Route 4 – Grand Canal Turistica
The same as Route 1, but with fewer stops. Only runs in high season.

Route 5 – Circolare
A circle line, both ways, going round the perimeter of the main body of Venice, including Murano to the north, and S. Giorgio Maggiore and La Giudecca to the south. The full circuit takes 1 hour 45 minutes.

Water Taxis
A luxurious way to travel. There are numerous taxi stands Always settle the price before embarking.

Traghetto
A gondola-type ferry from one side of the Grand Canal to the other. You ride it standing up, so be sure you have your 'sea legs'! Cost: 300 lire.

Gondolas
Gondola transport is picturesque but pricey. The gondoliers operate a scheduled tariff according to time or distance. Locals – and most tourists, once they've learnt the system – take the water-bus, which is far cheaper.

The problem is that the 500 remaining gondoliers of Venice can earn a living only during a six-months' tourism period, but want to feed their families year-round. There's just no alternative employment during off season. However, despite the cost, most visitors go at least once for a gondola ride – may be as part of a city tour, or on a moonlight Gondola Serenade. More expensive, try hiring one yourself – having agreed the price first – and sit back to enjoy a unique transport experience.

By official decree dated 1562, gondoliers may paint their 33-ft boats any colour they like, so long as it's black. The design is traditional, with origins going back to the 7th century AD. The craft weigh around 1500 lbs, and are deliberately skewed to counterbalance the tough problem of propelling and steering with only one oar.

Watch the steering. To stop his boat waltzing round and round, the gondolier uses a double stroke. The main drive comes from *pushing* on the oar. That sends the boat onwards, but swerving left. The return stroke is made under water, with blade almost flat. That swings the gondola to the right, rocking it gently. Progress is a mild series of zig-zags.

Despite the medieval setting, the 20th century still rears its head. Water-buses and taxis are fitted with hooters. Along the Rio Nuovo, where two canals cross, a policeman sits on point duty, working the traffic lights. Elsewhere are SLOW signs at tricky corners. Speed cops patrol in launches to check motorboat drivers whose wash causes erosion.

General rule of the canal is Keep Left. That is logical enough, for the gondola's one oar is always on the right. But there's a special Waterway Code for cornering. Stationed at the rear of a 33-ft boat, gondoliers must naturally corner blind. Whoever shouts first can swing out and take a corner wide, passing left or right. It all works, quite smoothly, no bad language.

2.3 Basic Venice

When John Ruskin wrote *The Stones of Venice*, he left not a stone uncovered. But the project of writing about virtually every significant building took him eight years to complete, from 1845 to 1853. For the modern tourist with less time to spare, here's a short list of Essential Venice, aimed at capturing the flavour of this fantastic City Without Roads.

(1) Take the standard tour of St Mark's and the Doges' Palace.
(2) Linger with a coffee or beer at an outdoor café on St Mark's Square, and hang the expense but mind the pigeons.
(3) Duck through the Clock Tower archway into the Merceria, and follow that narrow, winding shopping street through to Rialto Bridge.
(4) Try to remember some of Shylock's lines, as you cross the Rialto Bridge into the heart of the bubbling market area – always a trading centre since before the days of Shakespeare's *Merchant of Venice*.
(5) See the Grand Canal by slow water bus – oddly called the 'Accelerato' – 45 minutes with 15 bus-stops for 1500 lire. This journey is also top favourite for the jostle-and-pickpocket teams. Watch your purse or wallet, as well as the palaces!
(6) If you're desperate for a sandy-beach session, travel by waterbus across to the Lido where hotels charge steeply for access; or go to the free but scruffy public beaches at each end.

(7) Take a trip to the glass-manufacturing island of Murano, the lace-making of Burano, and to Torcello where the original Venice was established.

(8) One beautiful evening, embark on a Gondola Serenade.

(9) Schedule a morning visit to the Galleria dell'Accademia for the world's finest collection of Venetian paintings from 15th–18th centuries.

(10) Enjoy a wine-happy evening with musicians who perform all those Italian songs and light operatic favourites which grandma knew and loved.

Around St Mark's Square

All Venetian sightseeing starts at St Mark's Square, on foot. The essentials can be covered by the go-it-alone traveller with a guide-book. But you'd probably miss many of the details. It's worth taking a preliminary tour with a guide who has probably been doing the circuit for years, bringing the highlights to life. Just a reminder: modest dress is required for entry to the Cathedral – and, indeed, to other churches in Venice.

Here is Basic Venice, covered by the standard city walking tours:

Piazza San Marco

Napoleon called St Mark's Square 'the most splendid drawing-room in Europe'. The Piazza could easily win the popular vote for the world's most beautiful square. Paved with marble, this focal-point of Venice is about 190 yards long by 90 yards wide, with colonnades each side and enclosed at the end by the gorgeous facade of St Mark's.

Thousands of pigeons have traditional squatting-rights, and are fed at public expense. Peddlers sell bird-seed, and the pigeons earn their extra rations by perching on your shoulder or in your hair for that essential photograph with St Mark's in the background.

Expensive cafés with music enable you to enjoy the whole fabulous scene with flower sellers and instant-portrait artists, all in this wonderful setting of breathtaking architecture. In the arcades are shops with luxury merchandise to make you drool.

The Bell Tower (Campanile)

325 feet high, the Campanile dominates Piazza San Marco. It was completely rebuilt in 1912 after the original 1100-year-old building collapsed in 1802. There's a lift, if you can't face the climb on foot.

Open: Daily – Summer 10-22 hrs; Wintèr 10-16 hrs.

The Clock Tower (Torre dell'Orologio)

This 15th-century tower stands on St Mark's Square to the left of the Cathedral. Besides telling the time, the complicated clock face also shows phases of the moon and signs of the zodiac. You can climb to the roof for a magnificent viewpoint, where two bronze Moors will deafen you by hammering on the bell every hour. They have hammered out the time since 1497. The archway beneath is entrance to the main shopping street called Merceria, which zig-zags through to Rialto Bridge – well signposted along the way.

Saint Mark's Cathedral (Basilica de San Marco)

'The' great place to see in Venice – the Basilica built to enshrine the body of St Mark, stolen in 9th century from his tomb in Alexandria. It was a shrewd robbery, giving Venice great prestige, second only to Rome, and basis of a lucrative pilgrim trade. The present Greek-cross groundplan with five domes was built in 11th century. The magnificent golden mosaics were added in 12th and 13th centuries, with later dazzling upgrades by top Renaissance artists such as Titian and Tintoretto. Visit the Galleria above, for a closer view of the mosaics.

The interior is a treasure house, thanks partly to an edict dated 1075 that all Venetian trading vessels should bring back from their voyage something of value to enrich the Basilica. Hence the hundreds of rare marble columns, and items of alabaster and jasper. The Treasury is crammed with 4th-Crusade booty from Constantinople. Greek, Byzantine, medieval, Tuscan, Lombard and Venetian art have all left their mark, to make the Cathedral a sumptuous museum.

The golden altar-piece called the Pala d'Oro, encrusted with jewels and depicting scenes from St Mark's life, is the product of 500 years' of local craftsmanship. The famous four Bronze Horses on the terrace above the main door are copies. The originals – more loot from Constantinople – are inside the Cathedral, to protect them from 20th-century pollution.

Masses: Sunday at 7.00, 7.45, 8.30, 9.15 & 10.00 hrs.
Sung Mass: 11.15, 12.00 & 12.45 hrs.

The Piazzetta

This smaller square opens out from Piazza S. Marco onto the quayside which looks across to the island of S. Giorgio Maggiore. The Piazzetta has the Doges' Palace to one side, faced by the Libreria Vecchia on the other. The Old Library was rated by Palladio as the most beautiful building since antiquity. It houses the 'Library of St Mark', though the 700,000 volumes have overflowed into the adjoining Mint (Zecca).

The twin columns of St Theodore and St Mark were looted from Lebanon in 1125. The winged Lion of St Mark – universal symbol of Venetian power – probably came from Persia. According to Venetian superstition it's bad luck to walk between the two columns, where public executions formerly took place.

Doge's Palace (Palazzo Ducale)

Adjoining St Mark's Basilica is the former residence of the Doges, and seat of Government during the Venetian Republic. This is the most fantastic public residence of all time – a treasure house of Venetian painting, with every great Renaissance artist represented.

The Giants' Staircase is named after Sansovino's huge statues of Neptune and Mars, symbolising Venetian power on sea and land. Specially interesting are the private apartments of the Doges, and the massive 14th-century Hall of the Great Council, which could accommodate up to 1800 registered voters who could attend the Council sessions. Here's where all the big decisions were made.

Italy's finest artists all had a share in painting the Hall, though many originals were destroyed by fire in 1577. Tintoretto, Veronese, Bassano and Palma the Younger decorated the reconstructed building. Tintoretto's main contribution was *Paradise*, claimed as the world's largest oil painting, measuring 72 feet by 22.

In contrast to all this opulence, you can visit the dungeons and torture chambers which backed up the administration of justice.

Bridge of Sighs (Il Ponte dei Sospiri)

Walk along the side of the Doge's Palace, facing out to the Lagoon. Look down the first side-canal – Rio del Pallazo – and there's the famous Bridge of Sighs which connects the Doge's Palace with the prison across the canal. Among the most famous inmates was Casanova, who managed to escape.

2.4 *Other Sights in Venice*

What next, after you've seen the great highlights around St Mark's Square? There are dozens of museums and galleries to explore, an incredible 900 palaces to admire, and magnificent churches around every corner. All that, amid a visual feast which kept generations of artists busily painting the Venetian panorama for centuries ... With camera along the Grand Canal, you can repeat this scenic dream-world, quite unchanged, from the early 18th-century paintings of Canaletto.

For supplementary sightseeing, browse through the short-list below.

Museums & Galleries

Note: Opening times and closing days of Museums and Galleries in Venice are a law unto themselves. Before planning a visit, please check locally for the latest information and entrance fees.

Academy

Ponte dell'Accademia　　　　　　　　　Tel: 5222247
This museum ranks as one of the world's greatest collections of 14th–18th century Venetian painting. Make this gallery your top choice, if you cannot work round them all.
Open: Tuesday-Saturday 9-14; Sunday 9-19 hrs.
Closed: Monday.
Water Bus: 1, 2. Stop: No. 12 – Accademia.
Entrance: 4000 lire.

The Peggy Guggenheim Collection

Dorsoduro 701　　　　　　　　　　　Tel: 5206288
Palazzo Venier dei Leoni, on Grand Canal halfway between Santa Maria della Salute and the Accademia.

Houses a magnificent private collection of 20th century art, featuring Cubist, Abstract and Surrealist sculptures and paintings assembled by the American heiress. Most of the big 20th-century names are represented, though maybe not of the same incomparable quality of the Guggenheim in New York City.
Open: May-October, Monday-Friday 12-18 hrs.
Closed: Tuesday.
Water Bus: 1, 2. Stop: No. 12 – Accademia.
Entrance 5000 lire: free entrance Saturdays 18-21 hrs.

Ca' d'Oro and the Franchetti Gallery

Ca' d'Oro　　　　　　　　　　　　　Tel: 5238790
A miracle of 15th-century Venetian Gothic – a patrician dwelling, beautifully restored after flood damage. The palace houses the Galleria Franchetti collection of tapestries, sculptures and paintings, including works by Carpaccio, Titian and Van Dyck. From the first floor loggia, enjoy beautiful views of the Grand Canal.
Open: Tuesday-Saturday 9-13.30; Sunday 9-12 hrs.
Water Bus: 1. Stop: No. 6 – Ca' d'Oro

Scuola Grande di San Rocco

Campo San Rocco, next to the Frari　　Tel: 5234864
A 16th-century white marble building with its upper hall decorated by a magnificent cycle of paintings by Old and New Testament scenes by Tintoretto. Among other Tintorettos in the collection is his great masterpiece, the *Crucifixion*.
Open: Monday-Friday 9-13; 15.30-18.30 hrs. November-April 10-13 hrs only.
Water Bus: 1. Stop No. 10 – San Tomà
Entrance: 500 lire.

Scuola di San Giorgio della Schiavoni

Tel: 5228828
Castello 3259; on Calle dei Furlani – from Riva degli Schiavoni, at the fourth bridge up Rio della Pietà.

Well worth the effort of finding this former headquarters of Dalmatian traders. Ground floor exhibition of a series of early 16th-century paintings by Carpaccio, illustrating lives of three patron Saints of Dalmatia – George, Trifone and Jerome. The scenes vividly depict 16th-century life in the Venice region.
Open: Tuesday-Saturday 9.30-12.30; 15.30-18.30 hrs. Sunday 10.00-12.30 hrs.
Water Bus: 1, 2 or 5. Stop: No. 16 – San Zaccaria.
Entrance: 3000 lire.

Jewish Museum

Campo del Ghetto Nuova, Cannaregio   Tel: 715359
Notice that word 'ghetto'? It's the original Venetian word, used in its modern sense since 1555, when a Papal decree enforced the medieval principle of segregation into a defined city area. Napoleon lifted the restriction when he defeated the Venetian Republic in 1797. In this ancient centre – near the present-day railway station – were five synagogues, mostly Ashkenazi. The museum documents Jewish history in Venice since the time of original 11th-century settlement on the island of Giudecca. It also includes a wide variety of traditional Jewish art during the 17th to 19th centuries.
Open: 16 March-15 November: 10.00-12.30; 15.00-17.30 hrs.
16 November-15 March: 10.00-12.30 hrs.
Closed Saturday, Jewish holidays and Sunday afternoon.
Water Bus: 5. Stop: Ponte delle Guglie.
Entrance: 6000 lire.

Correr Museum

Piazza di San Marco   Tel: 5225625
Located at the opposite end of the Piazza from St Mark's Cathedral.

Contains documents, records and antique relics of the life of Venice from the 14th to the 18th centuries; and also a rich collection of paintings from 14th to 16th century. The museum's most famous work is 'Christ giving the keys to St Peter' by Lorenzo Veneziano. Here also is Carpaccio's *Two Venetian Ladies*, otherwise known as *The Courtesans*.
Open: Monday-Friday 10-16 hrs. Saturday 10-20 hrs; Sunday 9-20 hrs. Closed Tuesday.
Entrance: 3000 lire.

Museo del Risorgimento
800 Veneziano
Located on the second floor of Correr Museum (see previous entry).
   Covers the history of Venice from 700 AD to 1866 (the fall of the Republic).
Open: Monday-Saturday 10-16 hrs. Closed Tuesday. Sunday 9-12.30 hrs.

Modern Art Gallery (Palazzo Pesaro)
Santa Croce   Tel: 5227681
This gallery, housed in a 17th-century Venetian Baroque palace, features 19th and 20th century paintings by both Italian and foreign artists.
Open: Tuesday-Saturday 10-16; Sunday 09.30-12.30 hrs.
Water Bus: 1. Stop: No. 5 - S. Staè.

Museum of Oriental Art
Santa Croce Ca' Pesaro   Tel: 5241173
On the third floor of the Palazzo Pesaro (see previous entry).
   An excellent collection of oriental vases, furnishings, paintings, sculpture and weapons - mainly from China, Japan and India.
Open: Tuesday-Saturday 9-13.30; Sunday 9-12.30 hrs.
Water Bus: 1. Stop: No. 5 - S. Staè.
Entrance: 2000 lire.

Museum of the Settecento (Palazzo Rezzonico)
                                         Tel: 5224543
One of the most splendid examples of 18th-century Venetian Rococo style - a palace built by wealthy Genoese bankers called Rezzonico. The finest artists were commissioned for the decorations. Robert Browning died here in 1889, during a visit to his son, who had earlier bought the Palace (after marrying an American heiress). Furniture and paintings are all 18th century.
Open: Monday-Thursday 10.00-15.30; Saturday 10-20 hrs; Sunday 9-20 hrs. Closed Friday.
Water Bus: 1. Stop: No. 11 - Ca' Rezzonico.
Entrance: 3000 lire.

Museum of St Mark's Basilica
Piazza San Marco
The Marciano Museum is located on the upper floors of St Mark's Basilica, showing carpets and tapestries, religious ornaments and precious items which belong to the Basilica.
Open: Monday-Saturday 9.30-17.00 hrs.
Entrance: 500 lire.

Museum Fortuny
S Beneto 3780   Tel: 5200995
Set in the Gothic palace which belonged to the Pesaro family, the museum contains works by Mariano Fortuny, famed for Fortuny silks. The collection includes paintings, fabrics, furniture and photographs.
Open: Tuesday-Sunday 9-19 hrs.
Water Bus: 1. Stop: No. 9 – San Angelo.
Entrance: 5000 lire.

Museum of Icons and Hellenic Study
Castello 3412   Tel: 5226581
Housed in the Scuola di San Niccolò dei Greci, this museum contains the famous Greek codices which include three Byzantine gospels of the 13th and 14th century, 80 icons from the Byzantine period, and works of Cretan and Greek artists who settled in Venice.
Open: Monday-Saturday 9-13 hrs; 14-17 hrs; Sunday 9.00-12.30 hrs. Closed Tuesday.
Water Bus: 1, 2. Stop: No. 16 – San Zaccaria.
Entrance: 2000 lire.

Museum of Natural History
Fondaco dei Turchi, Santa Croce 1730   Tel: 5235885
A Grand Canal palace founded early 13th century. It later functioned as a tobacco warehouse and residence for Turkish traders, and was converted to a museum in 1880. Main attraction is the science room with two Basilisks (mythological animals made up of the parts of other animals). The Dinosaur room is a must.
Open: Tuesday-Saturday 9-13; Sunday 9-12 hrs.
Water Bus: 1. Stop: No. 3 – Riva di Biagio.
Entrance: 3000 lire.

Churches

Santa Maria della Salute
Built in thanksgiving for the ending of a plague in 1630, when 40,000 died in Venice alone. The plan is octagonal, and there are two huge domes. The sacristy contains twelve paintings by Titian, and the *Marriage at Cana* by Tintoretto.
Water Bus: 1. Stop: No. 14 – Salute.

Santa Maria Formosa
Located north of St Mark's, and due east of Rialto Bridge, on a lively square called Campo Santa Maria Formosa, with a regular morning fruit market.

    The church dates from the 7th century when the Virgin Mary is reputed to have appeared to the Venetians as a fully-formed lady (Formosa). The present church was rebuilt in 1492.

San Zanipolo (Santi Giovanni e Paolo)
Located a few blocks north again of Santa Maria Formosa (see above).
One of the finest Gothic churches in Venice. Contains a beautiful altarpiece by Giovanni Bellini, and four ceiling paintings by Veronese.

San Polo (San Paolo)
Campo di San Polo
One of the city's oldest churches. Contains several important works by famous Venetian artists, including Tintoretto and Tiepolo.
Water Bus: 1. Stop: No. 8 – San Silvestro.

San Giorgio Maggiore
Basilica on the island of San Giorgio Maggiore, built 1791 by Palladio. From the bell tower – lift available – there's a splendid view across to St Mark's Square. The church contains two Tintorettos.
Water Bus: 5, 8 from Zaccaria – one stop to S. Giorgio.

Santa Maria Gloriosa dei Frari
Campo San Rocco
A Franciscan Gothic-style church, built in 14th century. The campanile is the second highest in Venice. Many famous Venetians are buried here, including Titian. Over the High Altar is one of Titian's greatest religious paintings – the *Assumption*.
Water Bus: 1, 4. Stop: No. 10 – San Tomà.

Parks & Gardens

Giardinetti
Molo, Quay San Marco
This small park adds a touch of green, which is otherwise lacking in the city.

Giardini Pubblici (Public Gardens)
Riva dei sette Martiri
The gardens were laid out on the instructions of Napoleon 1, at the South East of the main island.

2.5 *Shopping in Venice*

Shopping for the standard tourist purchases is far easier in Venice than in other major cities.

Florence is best for leather; Milan for silk; and Rome or Naples for gloves. But all those specialities and other craft products like cameos or lace are available, in infinite variety, in the hundreds of stores that line the narrow streets of Venice. Comparison shopping is easy, with a dozen similar window-displays within a hundred yards. Haggling can bring price reductions, especially in late season when shopkeepers want to clear their shelves for the winter recess.

Venetian glass comes in wonderful, glittering array, with highest prices in the arcades of St Mark's Square itself. Best bargains are in small glassware shops away from the centre. It's fascinating to take a boat excursion to see glass-blowers at work on the island of Murano, but prices in the factory showrooms are not necessarily any cheaper. From street stalls you can often buy very low-cost figurines which are slightly sub-standard, with flaws that only an expert would detect.

Other interesting buys:

Leather – fabulous choice! The Venetians wear leather as if it were a second skin: jackets, trousers, skirts, shoes, gloves.
Masks – are a revival from the age of masked balls, a key part of Venetian culture. Banned for many years, masks are again hand-made specially for Carnival celebrations in February. In olden times, Venetian brides wore masks on their wedding day.
Silks – a great selection, including ties, scarves and shirts. The prints, patterns and colours are full of sunny Italy.
Lace – is mostly handmade in Burano, or specially imported from Korea or Taiwan. Try and tell the difference, apart from the price!

Shopping Areas

Opening hours: generally 9.00-12.30 and 15.00-19.30 hrs. Closed Sunday, and Monday morning.

San Marco area – The luxury end of Venetian trade is around the arcades of Piazza San Marco, and along the streets just west of the Piazza. Just look at the fabulous window displays, but don't dare ask the prices if you cannot stand shocks.

The Merceria – One of Europe's most famous shopping streets, following a narrow and zigzag route between St Mark's Square (starting from the archway below the Clock Tower) to the Rialto Bridge. Shops are full of designer clothes, including leather goods created by famous names such as Fendi, Armani, Gucci, Al Duca d'Aosto, Gianni Versace, Bussola . . .

The Rialto Bridge – The bridge itself, and the area just north, is crowded with tiny shops that sell jewellery, lace, handbags, gloves and many knick-knacks. Allow plenty of time for strolling.

Markets

Venetian markets are open generally from very early in the morning until about 14.00 hrs. Closed Sundays.

Rio Terra San Leonardo, over Ponte delle Guglie
A very colourful fruit and vegetable market, open daily.
Fabbriche Nuove, on Grand Canal, just north-west of Rialto.

This fishmarket is famous for its Adriatic seafood such as eels, crabs, scampi, octopus, mussels and sea bass.

Street Stalls are everywhere. The fruit and vegetable vendors sell melons, peaches, artichokes, grapes, mushrooms, oranges, and it's even possible to buy a five-kilo drum of Parmesan cheese.

2.6 *Eating Out in Venice*

Venetians are great food-lovers, and certainly like to take their time. Lunch or dinner can last at least two hours over three or more courses. For much of the year you can dine outdoors, enjoying both the food and what's happening around you. Excellent seafood is available everywhere, but is not necessarily cheap.

Although prices for à la carte meals can be rather high, there is usually a 'menu turistico' available which is generally good and inexpensive. Besides the pricier restaurants, there are many more modest places known as Tavola Calda, Rosticceria, or Fiaschetteria. Try them for a simple lunch!

Try Some Local Specialities

Fegato alla Veneziana – Calf's liver thinly sliced and cooked in butter with onions.
Baccalà alla Vicentina – Salt cod simmered in milk.
Polenta – Pudding of maize flour which can be accompanied by a variety of sauces, and served with game, mushrooms, sausages etc.
Risi e bisi – risotto with peas.
Regional Wines: Soave, Bardolino and Valpolicella.

Restaurant Suggestions

Price guideline

Prices in the listed restaurants may be subject to change; and obviously everyone orders differently. But here's the price grading system:

   £ = under £10, and frequently much less
   ££ = £10–£20
   £££ = £20+

Restaurants for Special Occasions

Antica Besseta Salizzada del Zusto, Giacomo dell'Orio   Tel: 721687
Home cooking and very few tourists. Reservations essential.   £££

Capri Corte Canal, Rio Marin   Tel: 718583
Venetian cuisine. Outside seating in summer, and sometimes music.   £££

Café Orientale Rio Marin, S. Polo 2426 Tel: 719804
Elegant and sophisticated, with canal terrace. Reservations advisable.   £££

La Corte Sconta Calle Pestrin Castello Tel: 5227024
'Hidden Courtyard', famous for fish dishes and Jewish pastries.   £££

Do Forni Calle Specchier, 468 San Marco
         Tel: 5237729
Expensive, but a jet-set favourite. The interior is a reconstruction of an Orient Express carriage. Closed Thursdays.   £££

Eating at Reasonable Prices – Trattorie

Al Gazebo Ponte delle Guglie 133a   Tel: 716380
Choose from the House Special Menu. From June till September you may dine outdoors. Closed Thursdays.   ££

Alla Borsa San Moise   Tel: 5238819
Offers a good tourist menu.   ££

La Zucca San Giacomo dell'Orio, Santa Croce
         Tel: 700462
Outside seating in summer. Many of the menu dishes are exclusive to this trattoria.   ££

Venexiana Cannaregio   Tel: 716269
A simple trattoria, serving an excellent fish soup.   ££

Alla Madonna Calle della Madonna, nr Rialto
         Tel: 5223824
Extremely busy fish restaurant.   ££

Burchielle Santa Croce 393   Tel: 5231342
A simple trattoria, very popular with the locals.   ££

Taverna San Trovaso Rio San Trovase, Dorsoduro   Tel: 5203703
Popular with locals. Everything from pizzas to 4-course meals.   ££

Rosa Rossa Calle della Mandola, San Marco 3709   Tel: 34605
Sister restaurant to Gazebo. Also specializes in fish dishes. Offers a 'House Special' menu.   ££

Zanze   Santa Croce 231   Tel: 5223555
Small, stylish, typically Venetian – a lovely restaurant off
the beaten track. Serves excellent fresh fish. Offers a
special-price menu.   ££

Pizzerias

There are lots of these scattered around Venice.

Ginos   Lista di Spagni   Tel: 716072
A popular meeting place, serving excellent pizzas and wine
from the Veneto region. Closed Thursday.   £

Da Sandro   Campiello Meloni, S. Polo   Tel: 5234894
Small but characteristic. The pizzas are excellent.   £

Alle Oche   S. Crose Campo San Giacomo Dall
'Orio (near Camposa Giacomo)   Tel: 5241161
Wonderful pizzas. Especially popular with young
people.   £

All' Capon   Campo Santa Margarita
Extremely good pizzas.   £

All Sportivo   Campo Santa Margarita   £

Cafés and Bars

Harry's Bar
St Mark's Square
Worth dropping in for an aperitif, as you can even pay for
your drink by American Express! Let the barman decide
which speciality is in season.

Café Florian
St Mark's Square
Opened in 1720, this is reputed to have been the first
coffee house in Europe. In the summer months, orchestras
play in St Mark's Square, once described by Napoleon as
'the drawing room of Europe'. The prices match the fame,
and a cup of coffee will cost a fortune. However, it is worth
the treat, for the view alone.

Quadri
Located on the other side of the square from the Café
Florian, almost as old and just as famous.

Harry's Dolci
773 di Sant' Eufemia (on the Guidecca) For the sweet-
toothed, it is sheer luxury! It's also possible to eat lunch or
dinner, followed by the cakes (dolci). They even serve
champagne from the pump!

Da Leoni
Hotel Londra, Riva degli Schiavoni
Upmarket cocktail bar with piano music. Set in a superb location, overlooking the lagoon.

2.7 Nightlife in Venice

It's Romance that balances the Venetian budget: the Romance of a medieval past, and of moonlight on the Lagoon. After dark, gondoliers light their coloured lanterns in readiness for the loving-couple trade. An hour of Venice by Night – along mysterious, dimly-lit canals, and preferably with music – is essential to any well-organised honeymoon.

That explains the comment of a sleepy tourist in Venice. 'Couldn't sleep a wink last night!' he complained. 'Nothing but gondoliers yowling their heads off, and playing banjoes!'

In one respect he was wrong. Gondoliers rarely sing. It's against their Union rules. If you want music with your gondola, you hire a singer and instrumentalist for the appropriate extra fee. On a personalised basis, that will cost a fortune. However, the cost can be kept within decent limits by taking a Gondola Serenade. Six persons to a gondola, a flotilla sets off, keeping close to another boat with the quota of musicians. Suggestion: take wine and paper cups with you, including supplies for the gondolier, and you could easily find he joins in the singing!

Certainly, after a full day of museums and churches, it's time to relax. In general, Venetian nightlife consists of eating late, and then sitting at an outdoor café, watching the world go by. If you want more action, certain restaurants offer night-time entertainment; and there's a handful of discotheques, or the Casino. At a more cultural level, the theatre offers a pleasant alternative: watch the posters for what's on.

Restaurants with Entertainment

Prices are usually quite high. Check them out before dining.

Antico Pignolo   Calle Specchieri 451

L'Arlecchino   Hotel Bauer Grünwald, San Moise 1440

Night Club Antico Martini   San Marco, Campo San Fantin 1980

Parco delle Rose   Lido

Blue Moon   Lido, Piazzale Sergher

Theatres

La Fenice San Fantin 2549 Tel: 25191
Goldoni Calle Goldoni Tel: 705838
Del Ridotto Calle Ca'Vallaresso, San Marco
 Tel: 22939
Malibran Cannaregio 5870

Casinos

During winter months (October to March) the Palazzo Vendramin houses the Venice Casino. It's here that Richard Wagner lived when he composed his opera *Tristan and Isolde*. Water bus No. 1, stop 4 (San Marcuolo).

In summer months (April to September) the casino operation moves to the Lido di Venezia, and is accessible on vaporetti Nos. 1 and 2, or by water bus No. 28 from Piazza San Marco or Piazzale Roma.

In both locations there are floorshows, restaurants and dancing. You can play roulette, chemin de fer, baccarat and blackjack. Remember to take your passport to gain admittance to the gambling rooms. Jacket and tie are required for gentlemen.

Open from 3 p.m. until 3 a.m. Entrance fee: 15,000 lire.

2.8 Sunday in Venice

Venice becomes very busy on a Sunday, as all the mainlanders come over to Venice for the 'Passeggiata' in their Sunday best. There are often special events happening in Venice on a Sunday – check once in Venice for details.

Excursions

A variety of excursions are available in Venice on a Sunday, so check once in Venice for details.

Shops

Most clothes shops are closed on a Sunday, but there are a large selection of gift shops open, selling Venetian glass or Burano lace. Most of the shops that are open are to be found around St Mark's Square, the Rialto Bridge, and near the Lista di Spagna – one of the more economical shopping areas.

Museums and Galleries

Almost all are open on a Sunday. See earlier chapters for details.

Church Services

Services are usually held in Italian, but occasionally the Church of St Moise behind St Mark's Square has a service in English.

The Basilica of St Mark's has a sung mass at 10.00 hrs.

The Anglican Church services are at 8.30 hrs. and 11.30 hrs. Mattins 10.30 hrs. This is to be found near the Accademia, at Campo San Vio 870.

2.9 At Your Service in Venice

Banks & Exchange Bureaux

General opening hours for banks are Monday-Friday 8.30-13.30 and 14.45-15.45 hrs.
Credito Italiano – Riva del Carbon, San Salvador 5058
        San Marco, Bocca di Piazza Ascensione
Banco San Marco – Santa Lucia Station F.S. 122
Cassa Di Risparmio Di Venezia – Centro Storico, Campo Manin
        Piazzale Roma, Santa Croce 458.

Exchange Bureaux & Banks Open Late

Ferrovia, Railway Station – Open daily 8-13 and 15-20 hrs. Various other exchange bureaux are scattered around the city, especially in the St Mark's Square area. They are usually closed Saturday afternoon and Sundays. However, it is often possible to change money at the hotel reception, at a less favourable rate.

Post Office & Telephone

Opening hours: 8-14 hrs. Monday-Saturday.

Main Post Office

Poste Centrali Rialto, Fondaco dei Tedeschi. The telegram office is open 24 hours a day.

Branch Offices

Lista di Spagna 233; and Campo San Stefano 2801.

Telephones

Long distance calls may be made from a S.I.P. office (pronounced 'seep'). This is a section of the Post Office, from which you can make phone calls at reasonable cost. The main S.I.P. office is near Rialto Bridge in the Campo San Bartolomeo, and it opens daily 8.30 till midnight. There's another S.I.P. office inside the Railway Station, and it's open daily 8-20 hours.

Marco Polo Airport also has a S.I.P. office in the main departure hall.

Emergency Phones

Police – Fire Brigade – Ambulance   Dial 113

Useful Telephone Numbers and Addresses

Police
Passport and Foreigners Dept., Castello 5053
Tel: 703222
If money or passport is stolen, report to this office and obtain a 'declaration of theft' – essential for any insurance claim.
There is a local police station in each section of the city.

First Aid
Piazza San Marco – open Monday-Saturday 8-20 hrs.
Tel: 5286346

Hospital – Casualty Departments
Ospedale al Mare (Lungomare d'Annunzio/Lido)
Tel: 761750
i Civili Rivuti di Venezia, Campo Santi Giovanni e Paulo
Tel: 705622

Pharmaceutical Chemists
Open: Monday-Friday 9-12.30; 15.30-19.15 hrs. Saturday 9-12.45 hrs.
There is a chemist in each district. Name and address of the night-chemist is always displayed on the door. Alternatively ring: 192.

Lost Property
For losses on public transport:
If lost on a vaporetto apply to the 'oggetti rinvenuti' office at the A.C.T.V. (stop number 9, San Angelo); or A.C.N.I.L. (City Public Transport).
For losses elswhere: Riva del Carbon, Pallazo Farsetti (City Hall), Campo San Luca.

Consulates
British Consulate, Dorsoduro 1051
(on Grand Canal, by Accademia Bridge)
Tel: 52 27207.
Nearest US Consulate is in Trieste, via Roma 9
Tel: (040) 68728.
Nearest Australian or Canadian Consulates are in Milan.

Chapter Three

Florence

3.1 Introduction

Florence is a remarkable city, with art treasures that are unparalleled anywhere in the world. It's a prosperous and bustling city of elegance and refinement – reflected in its 20th-century reputation for fashion, craftsmanship, antiques and culture. As the cradle of the Renaissance, the Tuscan capital is packed with the finest paintings and sculptures of that extraordinary 150-year period from 1400 to 1550 when Florence led a re-birth of European civilisation.

Let's just mention a few names of former residents who brought fame to Florence: Dante, Petrarch and Boccaccio, among the writers and poets; Giotto, Leonardo, Michelangelo and Botticelli among the dozens of world-class painters; Machiavelli among the political thinkers; three centuries of the Medici family. Their Tuscan dialect became today's purest textbook Italian, closest to the original Latin.

In its setting amid hills on the banks of River Arno, Florence has preserved her medieval and Renaissance heritage of great churches, palaces, statues and bridges. Most of those great names from the past could easily find their way around the present-day centre of Florence.

Finance for this rich golden age came from banking, and the wool and silk trade. In the 1420's, Florence had 72 operating banks which lent money and peddled influence throughout Italy and elsewhere in Europe. The enormous banking and merchant profits were ploughed into great mansions, furnished with luxury.

The dominant Medici family – first Giovanni (1360–1429) who founded the family fortune; then his son Cosimo the Elder (1389–1464) who became absolute ruler of the Florentine Republic; then a long line of successors – built great palaces and public monuments, and lavished money on the promotion of letters and the arts. The Medici name was everywhere.

So, above all, Florence is heaven for art-lovers. A seven-day city break can be filled with galleries every day, an embarrassment of artistic riches. Even then, it's impossible

44

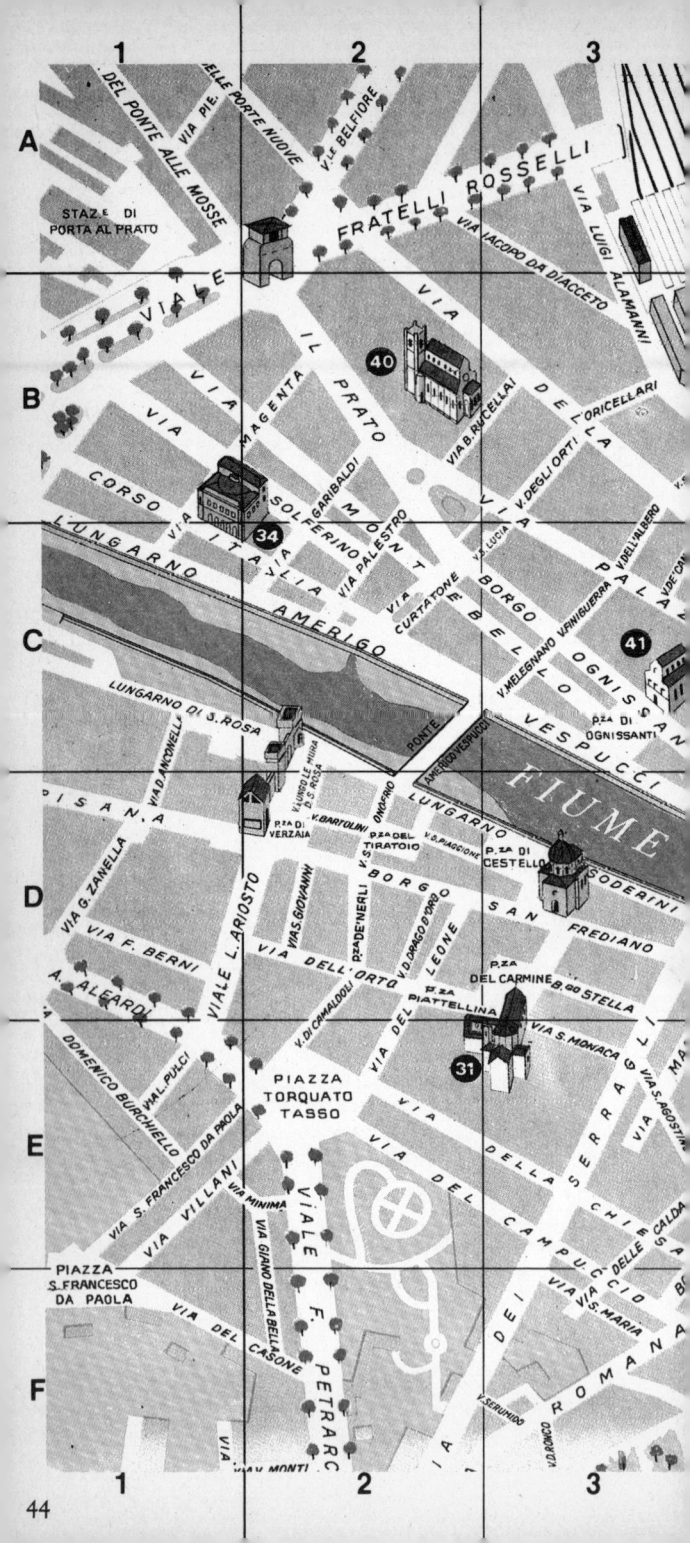

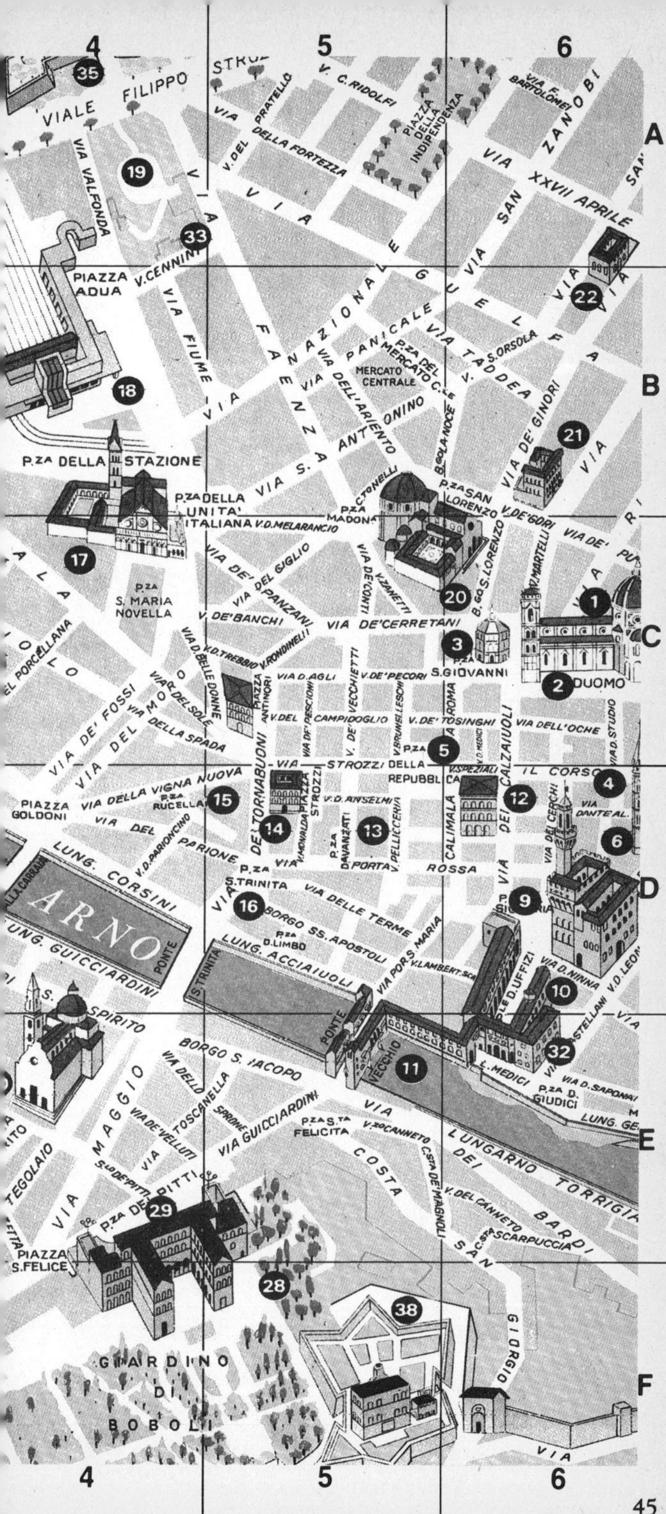
4
5
6
A
B
C
D
E
F
VIALE FILIPPO STROZZI
V. C. RIDOLFI
PIAZZA DELLA INDIPENDENZA
VIA F. BARTOLOMEI
VIA ZANOBI
VIA DEL PRATELLO
V. DEL
VIA DELLA FORTEZZA
VIA VALFONDA
VIA SAN ZANOBI
VIA XXVII APRILE
VIA
VIA NAZIONALE
VIA GUELFA
PIAZZA ADUA
V. CENNINI
VIA FIUME
VIA FAENZA
VIA PANICALE
P.ZA DEL MERCATO C.LE
MERCATO CENTRALE
VIA DELL'ARIENTO
VIA TADDEA
V. S. ORSOLA
VIA S. ANTONINO
B. GO LA NOCE
VIA DE' GINORI
P.ZA DELLA STAZIONE
P.ZA DELLA UNITA' ITALIANA
V. D. MELARANCIO
C. TONELLI
P.ZA MADONNA
P.ZA SAN LORENZO
V. DE' GORI
VIA DE' SERVI
VIA DEL GIGLIO
VIA DE' PANZANI
VIA DE' CONTI
V. ZANETTI
B. GO S. LORENZO
V. MARTELLI
P.ZA S. MARIA NOVELLA
V. DE' BANCHI
VIA DE' CERRETANI
VIA DEL PORCELLANA
V. D. TREBBIO
V. ROSINELLI
P.ZA S. GIOVANNI
DUOMO
VIA D. BELLE DONNE
VIA D. AGLI
V. DE' PECORI
PIAZZA ANTINORI
VIA DEL SOLE
VIA DE' FOSSI
VIA DEL MORO
DELLA SPADA
V. DEL CAMPIDOGLIO
V. DE' PESCIONI
V. DE' VECCHIETTI
V. BRUNELLESCHI
V. DE' TOSINGHI
VIA ROMA
VIA DEL CALZAIUOLI
VIA DELL'OCHE
V. D. STUDIO
V. D. MEDICI
VIA STROZZI
P.ZA DELLA REPUBBLICA
V. SPEZIALI
IL CORSO
PIAZZA GOLDONI
VIA DELLA VIGNA NUOVA
P.ZA RUCELLAI
VIA DEL PARIONCINO
VIA DEL PARIONE
VIA DEL TORNABUONI
V. MONALDA
PIAZZA STROZZI
V. D. ANSELMI
P.ZA DAVANZATI
V. PELLICCERIA
CALIMALA
VIA DEI CERCHI
VIA DANTE AL.
LUNG. CORSINI
ARNO
P.ZA S. TRINITA
VIA PORTA ROSSA
VIA DELLE TERME
P.ZA SIGNORIA
BORGO SS. APOSTOLI
P.ZA D. LIMBO
LUNG. GUICCIARDINI
PONTE
S. TRINITA
LUNG. ACCIAIUOLI
VIA POR S. MARIA
V. LAMBERT.
VIA D. UFFIZI
VIA D. NINNA
V. D. LEONI
V. CASTELLANI
S. SPIRITO
BORGO S. IACOPO
PONTE VECCHIO
L. MEDICI
P.ZA D. GIUDICI
VIA D. SAPONAI
LUNG. GE
VIA MAGGIO
VIA DELLO SPRONE
TOSCANELLA
VIA DE' VELLUTI
VIA GUICCIARDINI
P.ZA S.TA FELICITA
V. DEL CANNETO
COSTA
VIA LUNGARNO DEI TORRIGIANI
CSTA DE' MAGNOLI
BARDI
V. DEL CANNETO
C. STA SCARPUCCIA
SAN GIORGIO
P.ZA DE' PITTI
S. DE' PITTI
PIAZZA S. FELICE
TEGOLAIO
GIARDINO DI BOBOLI
VIA
1
2
3
4
5
6
9
10
11
12
13
14
15
16
17
18
19
20
21
22
28
29
32
33
35
38

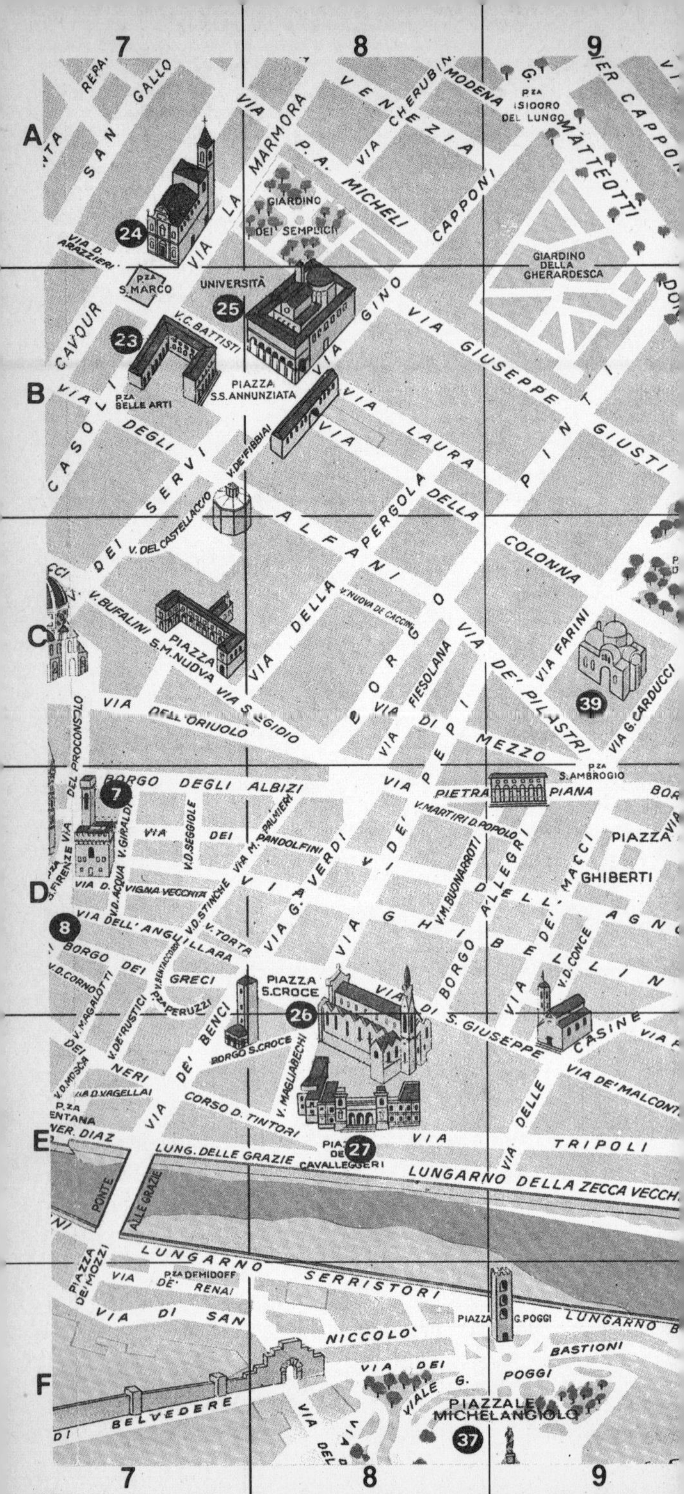
7
8
9
A
B
C
D
E
F
VIA REPA.
SAN GALLO
VIA LA MARMORA
VENEZIA
VIA CHERUBINI
MODENA
P.ZA ISIDORO DEL LUNGO
G. MATTEOTTI
VIALE CAPPONI
P. A. MICHELI
CAPPONI
GIARDINO DEI SEMPLICI
VIA D. ARAZZIERI
P.ZA S. MARCO
UNIVERSITÀ
CAVOUR
V. C. BATTISTI
PIAZZA S.S. ANNUNZIATA
P.ZA BELLE ARTI
VIA GINO
GIARDINO DELLA GHERARDESCA
VIA GIUSEPPE GIUSTI
VIA LAURA
VIA CASOLI
DEGLI SERVI
V. DE' FIBBIAI
PINTI
ALFANI
DELLA PERGOLA
DELLA COLONNA
V. DEL CASTELLACCIO
DEI
V. BUFALINI
PIAZZA S.M. NUOVA
VIA DELLA
V. NUOVA DE' CACCINI
BORGO
VIA FIESOLANA
VIA DE' PILASTRI
VIA FARINI
VIA G. CARDUCCI
VIA S. EGIDIO
VIA DELL'ORIUOLO
VIA DI MEZZO
VIA DEI PEPI
VIA DEL PROCONSOLO
P.ZA S. AMBROGIO
BORGO DEGLI ALBIZI
VIA PIETRA PIANA
V. MARTIRI D. POPOLO
VIA DEI PANDOLFINI
V. D. SEGGIOLE
VIA M. PALMIERI
V. G. GIRALDI
VIA FIRENZE
VIA D. VIGNA VECCHIA
V. D. ACQUA
V. D. STINCHE
VIA G. VERDI
V. M. BUONARROTI
BORGO ALLEGRI
VIA DEI MACCI
PIAZZA GHIBERTI
VIA GHIBELLINA
VIA DELL'AGNOLO
VIA DELL'ANGUILLARA
V. TORTA
BORGO DEI GRECI
V. D. CORNO
V. MAGALOTTI
V. DE' RUSTICI
V. BENTACCORDI
P. PERUZZI
PIAZZA S. CROCE
VIA DI S. GIUSEPPE
V. D. CONCE
CASINE
DEI NERI
VIA DE' BENCI
BORGO S. CROCE
V. MAGLIABECHI
V. D. MOSCA
VIA D. VAGELLAI
CORSO D. TINTORI
VIA DE' MALCONTENTI
VIA DELLE
P.ZA MENTANA
LUNG. ARMA DIAZ
PIAZZA DE' CAVALLEGGERI
VIA TRIPOLI
LUNG. DELLE GRAZIE
LUNGARNO DELLA ZECCA VECCHIA
PONTE ALLE GRAZIE
LUNGARNO SERRISTORI
PIAZZA DE' MOZZI
VIA DE' RENAI
P.ZA DEMIDOFF
VIA DI SAN NICCOLÒ
PIAZZA G. POGGI
LUNGARNO B
BASTIONI
VIA DEI POGGI
VIALE G. POGGI
VIA DI BELVEDERE
VIA DEL
PIAZZALE MICHELANGIOLO
24
25
23
7
8
26
27
39
37

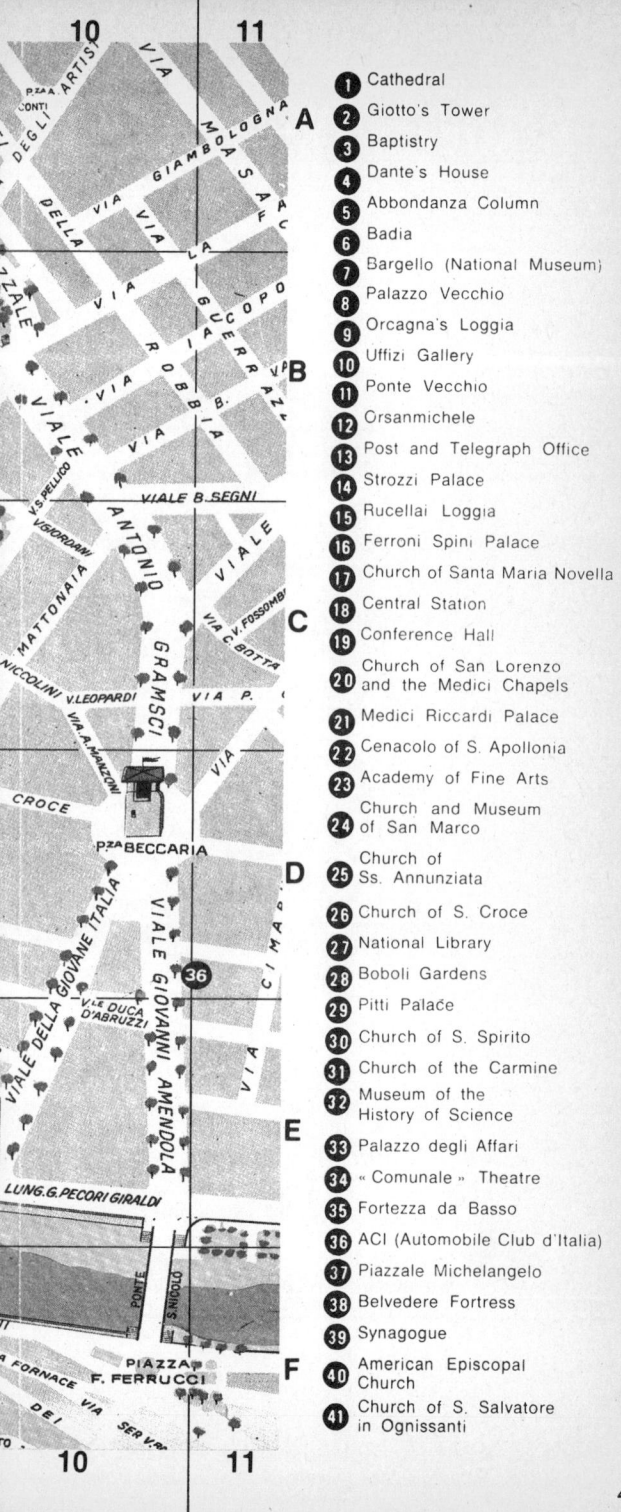

1. Cathedral
2. Giotto's Tower
3. Baptistry
4. Dante's House
5. Abbondanza Column
6. Badia
7. Bargello (National Museum)
8. Palazzo Vecchio
9. Orcagna's Loggia
10. Uffizi Gallery
11. Ponte Vecchio
12. Orsanmichele
13. Post and Telegraph Office
14. Strozzi Palace
15. Rucellai Loggia
16. Ferroni Spini Palace
17. Church of Santa Maria Novella
18. Central Station
19. Conference Hall
20. Church of San Lorenzo and the Medici Chapels
21. Medici Riccardi Palace
22. Cenacolo of S. Apollonia
23. Academy of Fine Arts
24. Church and Museum of San Marco
25. Church of Ss. Annunziata
26. Church of S. Croce
27. National Library
28. Boboli Gardens
29. Pitti Palace
30. Church of S. Spirito
31. Church of the Carmine
32. Museum of the History of Science
33. Palazzo degli Affari
34. « Comunale » Theatre
35. Fortezza da Basso
36. ACI (Automobile Club d'Italia)
37. Piazzale Michelangelo
38. Belvedere Fortress
39. Synagogue
40. American Episcopal Church
41. Church of S. Salvatore in Ognissanti

to do more than lightly skim the surface of these great collections.

For the less dedicated, two or three days is sufficient for Basic Florence. Don't wear yourself out with too many museums! Enjoy Florence as a good touring base. Take an afternoon excursion into the beautiful countryside of Tuscany, with its gently rolling hills, farmhouses, olive groves and cypress trees. There are famous spas to visit, such as Montecatini and Bagni di Lucca. You should definitely make time for sightseeing in Pisa or Siena.

Another popular idea is to split a week on a two-centre city break that links Florence with Rome or Venice. Florence is neatly located halfway between those two cities, with excellent train links in each direction. Reckon around 3½ hours either way, north or south.

The connecting rail journey itself is a delight, with good scenery to watch. Travel in Italian style, buying a bottle of wine and some paper cups to keep thirst at bay. En route between Florence and Venice, be alert for a halt at Bologna station. There, clued-up travellers lean out the window and buy piping-hot cartons of green lasagne from mobile trolleys that come dashing along. Delicious!

When to visit Florence? For a dedicated art lover who likes to savour paintings in tranquillity, it's seriously worth considering Florence in winter, with the eveningtime bonus of classical concerts or opera. Otherwise, spring or autumn are idyllic seasons for enjoyment of Florence and the surrounding countryside.

The July–August climate can be hot, but Florence is then at its liveliest with international visitors. During high summer you can find cooler evenings by attending the summer festival of music, ballet and drama at Fiesole – the hilltop location a few miles outside Florence.

Among the other annual events, high fashion shows – Italian and international – are held in March and October at the Pitti Palace. On Easter Day there's midday mass and fireworks – 'Explosion of the Cart' (*Scopio del Carro*) – at the Duomo. Something different for football fans: a 16th-century game of football, in medieval costume and no holds barred, in Piazza Signoria on June 24 and 28.

Certainly there's much more to Florence than trudging around the galleries!

3.2 Getting Around in Florence

The historic centre of Florence is very compact, and you can easily visit most of the principal sites on foot. Take a few minutes to study the map. From the Central Railway Station, the heart of Florence is tightly packed into a semi-circle that reaches to the River Arno. A ring of boulevards called the Viali marks the boundaries of the original walled city. Just about everything worth seeing north of the Arno is contained within that ring-road.

The most important bridge on the sightseeing circuit is Ponte Vecchio, which is the shortest route between Pitti Palace and Uffizi Gallery. Note the location of the other main sites – Piazza Signoria, the Cathedral and Santa Croce – and you have the orientation problem licked.

Depending on location of your hotel, you may need public transport into the centre: that is, to Stazione Centrale, the railway station. Otherwise, you'll hardly ever have any use of public transport, except possibly an occasional taxi.

Buses (autobus)

Florence is well served by a comprehensive bus network. Buy tickets at A.T.A.F. kiosks or at bars or tobacconists, tabaccaio, as they are not available on the buses. Cost is 600 lire for each journey. Save time and money by buying a block of 4, 8 or 12 tickets at once. When you board the bus – at the back – stamp your ticket in the red machine.

There's a Bus Information Office – A.T.A.F. – at 57r Piazza del Duomo, where you can get a useful free bus map. Tel: 21 23 01.

Useful Bus Routes:

No. 7 – to Fiesole
No. 13 – to Piazza Michelangelo
No. 16 – from Vittorio Veneto to the centre (Hotel Michelangelo)

Taxis

Taxis may be hailed in the street, but are often elusive. Go to the nearest main square and wait hopefully at the taxi stand. From a hotel or restaurant, the concierge or cashier can phone for a radio-cab. The magic phone numbers are 4390 or 4798.

Fares are metered, and there are supplements for suitcases (500 lire each); Sunday 1,000 lire; and 1,000 lire extra after 10 p.m. Tipping is about 10%.

3.3 *Basic Florence*

If you go overboard on art appreciation, then Florence will keep you going for months with its great galleries and churches. Otherwise, for the short-time visitor, here's a basic check-list for enjoyment of a brief stay.

(1) Feast your eyes in the Pitti Palace, followed by a stroll through the Boboli Gardens.
(2) On another day, visit Rooms 7-15 on second floor of the Uffizi Gallery.
(3) Explore the Cathedral – Duomo – and the adjoining buildings.

(4) Stroll around floodlit Florence, and pause for lengthy refreshment at an outdoor café.
(5) Shop-gaze for gold across Ponte Vecchio; or listen to street musicians there, at night.
(6) Break for classical music at the Teatro Comunale or elsewhere, according to seasonal programme.
(7) Watch craftsmen in workshops around Piazza S. Croce – leather, silverware, mosaics – and visit the Franciscan church.
(8) Eat a Florentine beefsteak – bistecca alla Fiorentina – with a bottle of Chianti.
(9) Visit the hill town of Fieseole by night, for summer-season musical events in the Roman Theatre.
(10) Spare an afternoon for a Pisa excursion, to check how the Leaning Tower is making out.

Most of Basic Florence is covered by the 'City Tour' offered by local travel agencies. It's better to take that half-day orientation tour, rather than wandering around on your own and possibly missing some of the great highlights. These tours normally visit the Piazza della Signoria; either the Pitti Palace or the Uffizi; the Cathedral area; the Accademia, mainly to see Michelangelo's *David*; Ponte Vecchio; Piazza Santa Croce; and the hilltop view of Florence from Piazzale Michelangelo.

Piazza Signoria

Here is the vivid centre of Florentine life for the past 1,000 years – scene of civic quarrels and festivities, overlooked by the high tower of Palazzo della Signoria (see section 3.4) from which the Piazza takes its name. The Piazza still remains the centre of Florentine political and commercial life, with the Palace used as Town Hall.

As you face towards the Palazzo della Signoria, a line of statues leads the eye towards the Uffizi, in the corner. Starting with the equestrian statue of Cosimo 1 in the centre of the Piazza, there's a Neptune Fountain by the corner wall of the Palace; dominated by the statues of Neptune and Hercules. The original Michelangelo's statue of David stood there from 1504 onwards, but was moved to the Accademia in 1873.

Next around the square is the open-plan Loggia dei Lanzi – a late 14th-century arcade built for public ceremonies, but now used as an open-air sculpture museum.

The Uffizi Gallery
Loggiato degli Uffizi 6   Tel: 218341
The building itself was designed in 1560 as government offices (*uffici*) on the orders of Cosimo 1. It stretches in two handsome wings from the Piazza della Signoria to the river. One wonders how many 20th-century civil service office blocks will give similar aesthetic pleasure, over 400 years later.

The Uffizi Gallery is rated as the finest in Italy, and also the world's most important for Italian painting – particularly Florentine. The basic collection was amassed by the Medici, with additions by the dukes of Lorraine. Later, more paintings came from Tuscan churches and convents which felt unable to look after their treasures properly. Many other works have been purchased or donated.

Every age of Italian art is represented. Masterpieces are displayed room by room mainly in date order, and in sequence of styles, schools and regions. In this logical order, you can appreciate how one master influences his pupils and successors; or you can jump direct to periods that interest you most. Best strategy is to see the Uffizi on a conducted tour, and then return at leisure direct to your favourite rooms. Many visitors concentrate on Rooms 7-15 on the 2nd floor.

Watch out for the 'Wild Boar' in the exit hall.
Open: Tuesday-Saturday 9-19 hrs; Sunday 9-13 hrs.
Entrance: 5,000 lire.

Ponte Vecchio

Crossing the River Arno at its narrowest point, the Ponte Vecchio – Old Bridge – was rebuilt in its present three-span form in 1345. The previous 10th-century bridge had been destroyed by flood; so the Ponte Vecchio was designed with durability in mind. It was solidly constructed to support two rows of shops, giving the bridge its present unique appearance of terraced houses with foundations in the river itself.

Originally those shops were fairly basic – tanners, butchers, blacksmiths, greengrocers. Then, in mid-16th century, the bridge moved up-market when a second-floor corridor was built to link the Palazzo Vecchio with the new grand-ducal Pitti Palace. In the cause of civic dignity, Ferdinand 1 in 1593 ordered out the 'vile trades', to be replaced by fifty goldsmiths and jewellers at double the rent. The shops were later extended over the river, with the back-developments supported by wooden beams.

Four centuries later, Ponte Vecchio is still a centre for the gold and jewellery trade, and more recently a nighttime venue for street musicians. Centre of the bridge is a bronze bust of Benvenuto Cellini, greatest of the Florentine goldsmiths.

Pitti Palace – The Palantine Gallery

Tel: 210323

Originally built by the Pitti family in 15th century to be one-up on their Medici rivals across the river, the Pitti Palace was finally acquired by the Medici dynasty in 1549, when the Pitti's fell on hard times. Many extensions were made over the following centuries, to make a fitting Medici ducal residence. Finally the Pitti Palace became a royal residence of the Savoia family (1865-71). Today the Pitti Palace houses several museums: the Palatine Gallery, the Silver Museum and the Modern Art Gallery (see next section).

In the Palatine Gallery, priceless paintings hang against a sumptuous gilt, stuccoed and frescoed decor, all left as placed by the last Medici and later Grand Dukes. The collection includes works by Botticelli, Raphael, Titian, Rubens, Velasquez and Murillo.

The Silver Museum

May also be visited on Wednesday, Friday and Saturday using the same ticket. It contains a rich collection of greatly-varied pieces made of gold, silver, ivory and amber. Here's the luxury craftsmanship which a family of unlimited wealth could buy during the 16th and 17th centuries.

Open: Tuesday-Saturday 9-14 hrs; Sunday 9-13 hrs.
Entrance: 4,000 lire.

The Cathedral Square

The Cathedral Square – Piazza del Duomo – is a very busy crossroads which has none of the tranquillity that usually goes with a religious centre. But here are three fascinating buildings which have attracted visitors for many centuries: the Baptistry, the Cathedral (Duomo) and the Bell Tower. Although different in style, each building is clad in contrasting slabs of black, white, green and pink marble to form a cheerful Florentine design.

Duomo – Cathedral Santa Maria del Fiore

The full grandeur of the Cathedral is best seen from a distance – from the hilltop of Piazzale Michelangelo across the river, for instance. The 13th-century assignment was to build a church which would out-rival anything produced by Pisa or Siena. Most of the building was completed by 1421. The architects were then faced with the baffling problem of crowning the Cathedral with a huge dome, of a size which was quite outside their technical experience.

The solution was worked out by Filippo Brunelleschi, who was a complete Renaissance man: painter, sculptor and goldsmith who also turned his hand to architecture. His cupola has delighted the world ever since. Among his other masterpieces in Florence are the Pazzi Chapel at Santa Croce, and the Pitti Palace.

The austere interior is a fine setting for the masterpieces it contains, including stained glass windows designed by Ghiberti and a clock decorated in 1443 with 'Heads of Prophets' by Paolo Uccello. The Pietà by Michelangelo is now located in the Cathedral Museum. (See next section).

Baptistry

Facing the Cathedral's main door, the Baptistry is reckoned to be the oldest building in Florence, on the site of a 5th-century church where originally stood something Roman, details unknown. The existing structure dates from 11th century, and was completed 200 years later. For a century it served as Florence cathedral. Drawing the crowds for the past 600 years are three magnificent gilded bronze doors.

Oldest is the South Door, with 28 panels designed by Andrea Pisano in 1330, of which the top 20 panels represent the life of John the Baptist.

The contract for the North door was awarded in 1402 to Lorenzo Ghiberti, following a competition in which five other leading artists including Brunelleschi also took part. The project occupied him and his collaborators – among them, Donatello and Uccello – for twenty years. The Florentine guilds who financed the work were so pleased with the result that they commissioned Ghiberti to do the East door as well. Ten framed squares depict Old Testament scenes, which took the Ghiberti team another thirty years to complete. Effectively, it set the seal on Florence as a major centre of sculpture, as well as painting. A century later, Michelangelo described that Baptistry door as 'the gate of Paradise'.

Giotto's Bell Tower, Piazza del Duomo (Campanile)

Standing alongside the Duomo, the Campanile designed by Giotto in 1334 is one of the great landmarks of Florence. Through its grace and harmony, the Bell Tower is considered to be the finest in Italy. It's well worth the climb of 414 steps for the splendid view of the city and of the Arno valley.
Open: Winter 9.00-17.30 hrs; Summer 9.00-19.30 hrs.
Entrance: 3000 lire.

The Academy Gallery (Galleria dell'Accademia)

Via Ricasoli 60   Tel: 214375
Is best known for its Michelangelo sculptures, including the original of *David* which stood in Piazza della Signoria until removed in 1873 as protection from the weather. This statue of Carrara marble permanently set Michelangelo's fame as one of the world's greatest sculptors. His four powerful but unfinished *Slaves* were intended for a papal mausoleum in Rome.

The Academy Gallery was created in 1784, and is devoted mainly to Florentine paintings of 13th to 16th centuries, with more recent additions of 18th and 19th century academic works.

Open: Tuesday-Saturday 9-14 hrs; Sunday 9-13 hrs.
Entrance: 4,000 lire.

Piazza Santa Croce

This square, with a statue of Dante standing there wrapped in a toga, has a considerable history as a craft centre. In the 14th century it was the heart of the dyeing and tanning trades, closely linked with Florentine prosperity from wool and leather manufacture. Leather and other crafts still flourish around the Piazza, greatly supported by tourist business.

Basilica of Santa Croce
Piazza S. Croce

Known as Italy's Westminster Abbey, the Gothic church of Santa Croce contains tombs and monuments to many of the great men of Florence: Dante, Michelangelo, Machiavelli, Galileo and Rossini. The largest and most famous Franciscan church in Italy, Santa Croce has rich decorations including frescoes by Giotto which had great influence on Florentine painters.

Cloisters lead to Brunelleschi's Pazzi Chapel and the Santa Croce Museum. (See next section)

3.4 Other Sights

In a three-night stay, you cannot expect to visit much more than Basic Florence. There is far more potential on a one-week visit, even if you make time for side-trips to Pisa or Siena. The Florentine museums, galleries and selection of churches combine into an art-lovers' paradise. Here's a short-list of the more outstanding sites to consider.

Museums & Galleries

State Museums close on Jan 1st, Easter Sunday, April 25th, May Day, June 2nd, August 15th, December 8th and Christmas Day.

Note: Entrance fees, opening times and closing days of Museums and Galleries are all liable to change. Specific rooms or even entire galleries are sometimes closed for restoration. Check locally for the latest information.

Try to avoid the crush in popular museums such as the Pitti Palace or the Uffizi. Weekdays, aim to enter around midday, when many visitors are ending their morning sightseeing. You'll then have a reasonably clear two hours before you go for a leisured lunch and siesta. Alternatively, arrive the moment the galleries open. Another good time to visit the Uffizi is after 16.30 hrs.

Palazzo Vecchio (Palazzo della Signoria)
Piazza Signoria   Tel: 27681
Ranking as the finest medieval building in Italy, the Palazzo della Signoria was founded in 1299 and was the early seat of government. This building, topped by a superb watch tower, witnessed many violent events in the city's history. As a centre of intrigue, the *cancelleria* was Machiavelli's office in the early years of the 16th century.

In 1540, the Medici ruler Cosimo 1 had the fortress-like Palazzo converted into his personal residence, suitably decorated with frescoes which paid fulsome tribute to himself and his ancestors. Afterwards, Cosimo 1 moved to the Pitti Palace, and this building became known as the Old Palace – Palazzo Vecchio. It is now used as City Hall.

With all that history in mind, the Palazzo Vecchio is worth a visit: particularly to see the great hall built in 1496, and the works of art on the 2nd floor.
Open: Monday-Friday 9-19 hrs; Sunday 8-13 hrs.
Closed: Saturday.
Entrance: 4,000 lire (free on Sunday, excluding special exhibition weekends when it is 6,000 lire).

Florence As It Used to Be (Museo di Firenze com'era)
Via dell'Oriuolo 4   Tel: 217305
An exhibition of paintings, prints and photographs relating to the city's physical history. This building was formerly a monastery.
Open: Monday-Saturday 9-14 hrs. (closed Thursday); Sunday 8-13 hrs.   Entrance 1,000 lire (free on Sunday)

Santa Maria Novella Cloisters
Piazza Santa Maria Novella, close to Central Station
                                                        Tel: 282187
The 'new' church dates from 1278, when Dominican monks replaced an earlier 10th century church. The stunning facade is green and white marble in Renaissance style, designed by Leon Battista Alberti.

The Cloisters give access to the Spanish Chapel, decorated around 1366 by Andrea da Firenze and his assistants as a tribute to the Dominican Order.
Open: Monday-Saturday 9-19 hrs. (closed Friday); Sunday 8-13 hrs.   Entrance: 3,000 lire

Innocenti Gallery
Galleria dello Spedale degli Innocenti
Piazza SS. Annunziata 12   Tel: 243670
Collection of pictures, sculptures, miniatures and furniture dating from the 14th to 18th centuries.
Open: Winter 9-13 hrs. (closed Wednesday); Summer (June–October) 9-19 hrs.   Entrance: 2,000 lire

Gallery of Modern Art
Piazza dei Pitti　　　　　　　　　　　　　Tel: 287096
On the second floor of the Pitti Palace, the modern art collection is housed in some 30 rooms. Discover the exciting Macchiaioli ('blotch painters'), Tuscany's own Impressionist movement of the 1860's – see rooms 23-26.
Open: Tuesday-Saturday 9-14 hrs; Sunday 9-13 hrs.
Entrance: 4,000 lire.

Bardini Museum & Corsi Gallery
Piazza di Mozzi　　　　　　　　　　　　Tel: 296749
Donated in 1923 by Stefano Bardini, a wealthy art dealer – a 20-room collection of wood, plaster and terra-cotta sculptures from Etruscan times to medieval; also 17th-century Florentine tapestries.
Open: Monday-Saturday 9-14 hrs (closed Wednesday); Sunday 8-13 hrs. (closed certain holidays, please check).
Entrance: 2,000 lire (free on Sunday)

Anthropology Museum
Via del Proconsolo 12　　　　　　　　　Tel: 296449
A worldwide collection of ethnic interest.
Open: First and third Sunday of the month 9-13 hrs.
Entrance: Free.

History of Science Museum
Piazza dei Guidici 1　　　　　　　　　　Tel: 293493
From an alchemist's laboratory to the telescope with which Galileo discovered the four 'Medici satellites' of Jupiter.
Open: 9.30-13 hrs & 14-17 hrs. Closed Tuesday, Thursday, Saturday p.m., Sunday and public holidays.
Entrance: 5,000 lire.

Michelangelo Museum – Casa Buonarroti
Via Ghibellina 70　　　　　　　　　　　Tel: 241752
Michelangelo bought the house for his nephew, Leonardo di Buonarotti, but never lived in it himself. Leonardo's son, Michelangelo the Younger, decorated the house and turned it into a memorial to the great artist.
Open: Monday-Saturday 9-14 hrs. (closed Tuesday); Sunday 9-13 hrs.
Entrance: 4,000 lire.

Santa Croce Museum (Museo Cimabue)
Piazza S. Croce 16　　　　　　　　　　　Tel: 244619
Includes works from artists such as Donatello, Cimabue, Veneziano, de Banco and Gaddi.
Open: Winter 10.00-12.30 and 14.30-17.00 hrs. (closed Wednesday); Summer (March 1–October 30) 10.00-12.30 hrs and 14.30-18.30 hrs.
Entrance: 2,000 lire.

Cathedral Museum (Museo dell'Opera del Duomo)
Tel: 213229

Piazza del Duomo 9 – behind the apse of the Cathedral
The museum contains many works of art – sculpture, articles in gold, silver, embroidery etc – which were created to furnish the Cathedral, Campanile and Baptistry, but could not remain for security reasons. The Pietà is one of Michelangelo's last works, carved when he was 75 years old, and planned for his own tomb.
Open: Summer – 9-20 hrs; Winter – 9-18 hrs; Sunday 10-13 hrs.
Entrance: 3,000 lire; free on Sunday.

National Sculpture Museum – Il Bargello
Via del Proconsolo   Tel: 210801
Built as a town hall in 1255, the palace later became the residence of the Captain of Justice (Bargello). As police headquarters, part of the building was used for torture and executions. Since 1859 the Bargello has served as the National Sculpture Museum, with medieval and Renaissance masterpieces, and ceramics, coins, arms and armour.
Open: Tuesday-Saturday 9-14 hrs; Sunday 9-13 hrs.
Entrance: 3,000 lire.

San Marco Museum
Piazza S. Marco   Tel: 210741
This Dominican monastery, rebuilt and decorated in 15th century, was focal point of Florentine culture throughout the Renaissance. In the 1490's, San Marco was the turbulent centre of religious fervour inspired by Savonarola, the demagogue Prior of San Marco.

Since 1869 this building has served like a one-man exhibition centre for the works of Fra Angelico and his pupils: panel paintings from other churches and galleries, his *Annunciation*, and particularly the frescoes in 44 dormitory cells, painted by the friar and his assistants. Among the other works are paintings by Fra Bartolomeo.
Open: Tuesday-Saturday 9-14 hrs; Sunday 9-13 hrs.
Entrance: 3,000 lire.

The Medici Chapels
Piazza di Madonna degli Aldobrandini, behind the church of S. Lorenzo   Tel: 213206
The New Sacristy was designed by Michelangelo in 1524. Most of the Medici Grand Dukes, and members of their families, are buried here, glorified in masterpieces of sculpture.
Open: Tuesday-Saturday 9-14 hrs; Sunday 9-13 hrs.
Entrance: 4,350 lire.

Archaeological Museum

Via della Colonna 36 Tel: 2478641
In the 17th-century Palazzo della Crocetta, the museum houses an outstanding collection of Egyptian, Etruscan and Greco-Roman finds.
Open: Tuesday-Saturday 9-14 hrs; Sunday 9-13 hrs.
Entrance: 3,000 lire.

Churches

Generally open until 12.30 and reopen at 15.00 hrs.

Orsanmichele

Via dei Calzaiuoli
Originally a grain market, converted into a church from 1380, with upper floors used for emergency grain stores. In early 15th century, 21 of the Florentine guilds each supplied a statue of their patron saint, with several of the commissions going to Ghiberti and to Donatello.

All Saints' Church (Church of Ognissanti)

Founded in mid-13th century, the church was re-done in Baroque style in 17th century. This church was the burial place of the family of Amerigo Vespucci, the Florentine explorer who gave his name to America. A fresco painted about 1470 – *Madonna of Mercy Sheltering the Vespucci Family* – includes a reputed portrait of Amerigo as a lad. A family tombstone is left of the altar.

The explorer was born in 1454 in the family home, Palazzo Vespucci, which is located close by in Borgo Ognissanti.

Church of Santo Spirito

Piazza Santo Spirito
Designed by Filippo Brunelleschi, this typical 15th-century Renaissance church is rich in art treasures – though many of the original works from the 39 semi-circular chapels have been removed to museums.

Church of the Carmine (Santa Maria del Carmine)

Piazza del Carmine
Worth visiting to see frescoes in the Brancacci Chapel, mostly painted around 1425–1428 by a young genius named Masaccio. Although only 27 when he died, Masaccio's work had enormous influence on the greatest of Renaissance painters – Michelangelo included – who closely studied his pioneer techniques of depicting space and perspective.

The most famous of the seven frescoes by Masaccio is 'Payment of the Tribute by Christ'.

Santa Trinità
Piazza Santa Trinità
Eleventh century church erected by the Vallombrosan Monks.

San Miniato Al Monte
Monte alle Croci
One of the most beautiful Romanesque churches in Italy, San Miniato was built in 11th century, and decorated in Florentine style with a green and white marble facade. Mosaics were added in 13th century and restored in the 19th. From its hilltop site, the visitor has a splendid view over Florence.

The Synagogue
Via Farani 4
The building is in pure Moorish style.

Parks & Gardens

Boboli Gardens
Pitti Palace Tel: 213440
An Italian court garden of cypress and hedge-lined alleys, with unusual statuary, grottoes and fountains.
Open daily: November-February 9-17 hrs, March, April October 9-18 hrs, May-September 9-19 hrs.

Botanical Gardens & Museum
Via Micheli 3 Tel: 284696
Open: Monday, Wednesday & Friday 9-12 hrs.

Other Places of Interest

Viewpoints

Among the delights of Florence is that there are numerous vantage points which offer breathtaking views of the city. Here are three of the most outstanding:

Giotto's Bell Tower – the Campanile
(See section 3.3)

Piazzale Michelangelo
Usually included on city sightseeing tours. From this Piazza on a hillside some 300 feet above the Arno, there's a classic view over the whole of Florence and out to the hills of Tuscany. Left to right, the city view takes in the church tower of S. Maria Novella, the bell-tower of Palazzo Vecchio, the whole side of the Duomo with its splendid cupola and adjoining Campanile, and the Basilica of Santa Croce.

In the centre of the square is a copy of Michelangelo's

David, and of his statues symbolising Day, Night, Dawn and Dusk.

Fiesole (north of Florence)

Usually included on city sightseeing tours.

On a hillside five miles outside Florence, Fiesole was an Etruscan settlement, then a Roman municipality dating from the first century BC. The bus-ride is delightful, winding up a hill bordered with beautiful gardens and villas and finally running into the central square. A music and film festival is held July–August in the 1st-century BC Roman theatre, with audience capacity of 3000.

Interesting & Free!

Casa di Dante

Via S. Margherita 1   Tel: 283343

Here are the reconstructed houses which belonged to the Alighieri family. Dante Alighieri, greatest of Italian poets, was born here in 1265. A small museum displays reproductions of Botticelli's illustrations for Dante's work, and portraits of the poet.

Open: Summer 9.30-12.30 hrs; 15.30 18.30 hrs; Winter 9.30-12.30 hrs; 15.30-18.30; Sunday 9.30-12.30 hrs; Closed Wednesday.

Palazzo Medici-Riccardi

Via Cavour 1

The palace was built 1444–1464 by the Medici family, who used it as their residence until they moved in 1537 to the Palazzo Vecchio. This style of palace architecture became the standard for other wealthy families during the height of Florentine prosperity. Visit the tiny family chapel to see Benozzo Gozzoli's fresco *Procession of the Magi*. Painted in 1459, all members of the family are right there, and anyone else who counted in Florence at that time!

Open: Monday-Saturday 9-12 hrs; 15-17 hrs; Sunday 9-12; closed Wednesday.

3.5 Take a Trip from Florence

Although Florence is so packed with city-centre interest, try to make time to see something of the Tuscan countryside. Due west is Pisa, only an hour away, to make first choice as an afternoon coach excursion. Due south is the beautifully-preserved medieval town of Siena, which demands a full day to appreciate the rolling Chianti hills and vineyards en route.

Pisa

Everything focuses on the 'Miracle Square': the Romanesque Cathedral, the Baptistry and of course the Leaning Tower. This unique group of buildings has survived since the 12th century – witness to the former power and prosperity of the ancient Maritime Republic which once rivalled Venice and Genoa. With its shallow natural harbour at the mouth of the River Arno, Pisa's bad luck was that the sea retreated from 13th century onwards. Pisa progressively declined as the harbour silted up.

But Pisa's reputation as a university town has remained intact, particularly strong in science ever since the stirring times when Galileo lectured here. In the Cathedral hangs the swinging bronze lamp which first set Galileo's mind working in 1581 on the mathematics of pendulum movement. Ten years later, he used the Leaning Tower for his famous demonstration that objects with different weights fall with identical velocity.

Scientific matters apart, the Cathedral is forested with Corinthian columns. An early 14th-century pulpit by Giovanni Pisano is a masterpiece of sculpture, with panels that depict New Testament scenes. Look also at the 16th-century bronze doors.

Cemeteries don't usually rate high on sightseeing itineraries, but it's worth visiting the walled Camposanto behind the cathedral. Although badly war-damaged in 1944, the cemetery is famed for its frescoes and sculptures.

The Leaning Tower is in no immediate danger, despite tilting 15 feet out of plumb. Climb 294 steps up a spiral staircase for a great view over the cathedral roof.

Siena

Inside the original city walls is medieval perfection, with a street plan virtually unchanged from 13th century. Buildings are the colour of burnt sienna from bricks made of local red clay. Motor traffic is banned from the centre – a maze of winding streets that finally empty into the principal Piazza del Campo.

The Campo, fan-shaped like a shell, offers a truly theatrical setting for the traditional *Palio* horse race, bareback and in medieval costume. The contest has been an integral part of the Siena calendar for centuries, based on intense rivalry between the 17 *contrada* or wards into which the city has been divided since medieval times. The race is held on July 2, with a repeat performance on August 16. Tickets are very expensive and difficult to obtain, but you can often see rehearsals on the previous days.

However, if you cannot make those dates, Siena is still a fantastic city to visit. You could spend your time entirely in the Campo, enjoying what could easily rate as the most beautiful square in Italy. Among the buildings to visit are the Cathedral, the Town Hall, and the rival Dominican and Franciscan Churches of San Domenico and San Francesco.

San Gimignano

Well-organised coach tours to Siena often include a visit to San Gimignano – another superb medieval survival, from which happily all 20th-century traffic is excluded. There are charming old streets and squares and towers, little changed from the 14th century.

3.6 Shopping in Florence

Florence is a good shopping city. The main craft centre is around the Piazza Santa Croce, with numerous leather and silver workshops. Jewellery stores are grouped on, and around, Ponte Vecchio. And there are world-famed fashion houses, shoe and knitwear stores, in the central shopping streets. In fact, Florentine fashion is as highly renowned as Parisian. The city is crammed with hundreds of fascinating little boutiques. Whether you wish to spoil yourself or not, window shopping in Florence is a delight!

Opening hours follow the normal Italian pattern: Summer: 9-13 hrs; 16-20 hrs; Winter: 9-13 hrs; 15.30-19.30 hrs. From 15 June-15 September, shops close on Saturday afternoon; during the rest of the year, on Monday morning. Food shops close on Wednesday afternoons.

Interesting Buys

Jewellery	– Gold & silver can be surprisingly cheap in Florence, though the more creative the item, the more expensive it is. Look for pill-boxes, napkin rings, photo frames and candlesticks.
Glassware	– Attractive, functional glassware, often very reasonably priced, is available from Empoli or Pisa.
Leather	– This is exquisite! Best buys are gloves, belts, purses, wallets and boxes of all shapes and sizes. It is often possible to have your initials stamped in gold leaf on any purchase.
Antiques	– These abound, and are invariably pricey. Bric-a-brac is practically non-existent.

Shopping Areas

Fashion Boutiques	– Via de'Tornabuoni, Via de'Calzaiuouli (smart and expensive).
Leather	– San Lorenzo, Santa Croce (Don't miss the leather school tucked away behind Santa Croce's sacristy in former Franciscan monks' cells).
Gold & Silver	– Ponte Vecchio.
Inlays & Mosaics	– Lungarno Torrigiani, Via Guicciardini, Piazza Santa Croce.

Antiques	– Borgo Ognissanti, San Jacopo, Via della Vigna Nuova, Via della Spada, Piazza del Duomo.

Other areas worth visiting are:

Via Strozzi Via Porta Rossa
Via Roma Via del Parione
Via dei Pecori Piazza della Repubblica

Shops

These are inevitably too numerous to list, but for quality goods at reasonable prices try:

Leather at 'Fibbi', Corsa dei Tintori 19/12.
Open 9-19 hrs daily. Closed on Sundays December–February.
Gold & Silver, 18 KT, Via S. Giuseppe 32r, Santa Croce.
All items are sold by weight and carry 18 carat hallmark.

Markets

San Lorenzo
Piazza San Lorenzo
Everything from mouth-watering fresh food to crocodile skin handbags! Prices are often reasonable, and some stalls accept credit cards and traveller's cheques.

Mercato Nuovo (Flea Market)
A score of stalls offering straw bags, sun hats, trinkets, jewellery, etc.

Piazza dei Ciompi (Flea Market)
Open daily in full season. Many interesting bits and pieces.

Mercato Cascine
Located in Cascine Park. Sells everything.

3.7 *Eating Out in Florence*

Living to eat – not eating to live – is part of the Tuscan way of life. Florentines prefer simple 'country' fare, and are somewhat unadventurous about exotic dishes from other countries. However, Italy is rich enough with its own superbly fresh local fruit and vegetables. You have no need to look further afield to eat well.

Typical Tuscan Specialities

Antipasto
Finocchiona	– A kind of salami flavoured with fennel seeds

Crostini	– Open chopped liver sandwiches

First Course

Ribollita	– A thick bread and vegetable soup
Cacciucco alla Livornese	– Fish stew with a very hot sauce
Pappardelle alla Lepre	– Pasta with hare sauce
Tortino di Carciofi	– Baked artichoke pie
Baccala alla Livornese	– Salt cod cooked in tomatoes, black olives and black pepper

Main Course

Bistecca alla Fiorentina	– A tasty steak which weighs about a kilo, and is enough for 2 people. Make sure to be very hungry, before ordering! Steaks are priced by weight – multiples of 'etto', which is 100 grammes (4 ounces)
Arista	– Herb flavoured roast pork
Stracotto	– Beef lengthily cooked in red wine
Trippa	– Tripe cooked in tomatoes and onions

Side Dishes

Fagioli al fiasco	– Beans cooked in a glass flask
Fagioli all'Uccelletto	– Haricot beans cooked with tomatoes, sage and garlic
Frittura mista	– Batter fried zucchini (courgettes), artichokes and other seasonal vegetables

Desserts

Zuccoto	– Ice cream cake
Panforte	– Chewy cake made in Siena with honey, candied fruits, cloves and almonds. A good cake to take home
Castagnaccio	– Cake made with chestnuts, pine nuts and sultanas
Torrone	– Nougat

Late Night Snack

The Florentines love a late-night spaghetti pasta dish washed down by lots of Chianti wine, followed by 'biscotti di Prato' – cookies from Prato dipped in Vin Santo, a sweet type of sherry used at the altar at Mass.

Tuscan Wines

A small hill area near Florence is called Chianti. It's from these hillsides that the renowned red Chianti wine is produced. Also try regional wines such as Vernaccia, Aleatico, Brunello di Montalcino and Nobile di Montepulciano.

Restaurant Suggestions
Price Guideline

Prices in the listed restaurants may be subject to change; and obviously everyone orders differently. But here's the price grading system:

£	= under £10, and frequently much less
££	= £10–£20
£££	= £21–£25

NOTE: For street addresses, there are two numbering systems in Florence. Red are for businesses, and black for private houses. Thus, 96/r = 96 rosso (red), which will be nowhere near 96 'black'. Watch it!

Restaurants for Special Occasions

It is advisable with all these restaurants to make a phone reservation, to avoid disappointment.

La Loggia   Piazzale Michaelangelo   Tel: 2342832
Dine outside on the terrace in the summer months.   £££

Paoli   Via dei Tavoloni   Tel: 216215
Old Florentine palace with frescoes & flowers. For 'special' treatment, speak to Benito the boss. Closed Tuesdays.   ££

La Posta   Via de'Lamberti   Tel: 212701
Just the place, if you like fish and a good selection of desserts. Closed Tuesdays.   ££

Da Noi   Via Fiesolana   Tel: 242917
Intimate atmosphere. Friendly assistance given by Sabina and Bruno. Booking essential. Closed Sundays and Mondays.   £££

Il Bargello   Piazza della Signoria   Tel: 214071
Wholesome Tuscan cooking plus international fare. Closed Mondays.   ££

Eating at Reasonable Prices

Guibbe Rosse   Piazza della Repubblica 13   Tel: 212280
Try their renowned 'Scaloppine alla Chiantigiana' – a secret recipe for escalope of veal in a Chianti based sauce. Delicious! From May–October you can dine outdoors.   ££

Pepe Verde   17 Piazza Mercato Centrale   Tel: 283906
Menu available in English. Closed Tuesdays.   £

Trattoria Mossacce   55 Via Proconsolo Tel: 294361
A tourist menu on request. Closed Sundays.   £

Ristorante Spada   62 Via della Spada   Tel: 218757
Menu available in English. Closed Sundays.   £

Pizzeria/ristorante Vecchia Carlino
15/17 Via Fratelli Rosselli   Tel: 353678
Good selection of Tuscan food, and excellent pizzas in the evenings. Closed Mondays.   £

Da Nello   56 Borgo Pinti   Tel: 2478410
Good selection of meat and fish.   £

Yellow Bar   Via Proconsolo 39/r
Excellent pizza and pasta. Open evenings only. Closed Tuesdays.   £

La Maremmana   Via Macci 77/r   Tel: 241226
Speciality Pasta alla Scoglio (Pasta with seafood). Closed Sundays.   £

Le Follie   Lugarno del Tempio 50   Tel: 677693
Pizzeria & Restaurant. Closed Tuesdays.   £

La Burrasca   Via Panicale
Excellent Pasta.   £

Diletto   Via Aretina 92/r   Tel: 678391
Closed Sunday.   £

Osteria del Cinghiale Bianco
Borgo S. Jacopo 43/r   Tel: 215706
Tuscan specialities. Closed Wednesday.   £

Tuscan Eating

Da Pennello   4 Via Dante Alghieri   Tel: 294848
Have an appetite! Closed Sundays & Mondays.   ££

Leo in Santa Croce   7 Via Torta   Tel: 210829
Try Leo's 'crostoni'. Closed Sundays.   ££

La Barcaccia   Corner of Via Verdi and
Via Lavatoi   Tel: 283958
Try the Fiorentina steak – one suffices for two persons.
Closed Tuesdays.   ££

Il Latini   Via Palchetti 6/r   Tel: 210916
Go early. Be as hungry as a lion. Closed Mondays.   ££

Armando   140 Via Borgo Ognissanti   Tel: 216219
Very pleasant atmosphere besides good food. Closed Wednesdays.   ££

Il Profeta   93/r Via Borgo Ognissanti   Tel: 212265
Excellent service and good food. Closed Sundays.   £££

Baldini Trattoria Via il Prato 96/r   Tel: 287663
Closed Saturdays and Sundays.   £££

Cantinone del Gallo Nero
Via S. Spirito 6/r   Tel: 218898
Typical Tuscan food. Closed Mondays.   £

Trattoria Tito Via San Gallo 112/r
Typical Tuscan trattoria. Closed Sundays.   £

L'Orologio Piazza Ferrucci 5/r   Tel: 6811729
Good Tuscan food. Closed Sundays.   £

Fish Restaurants

Trattoria Vittoria 52 Via Fonderia (corner
Ponte Vittoria)   Tel: 225757
Closed Wednesdays.   £££

Pierot 25 Piazza Gaddi   Tel: 702100
Closed Sundays.   ££

NOTE: In the above two restaurants, prices depend upon which seafood you choose, as fresh fish is sold by weight. The unit 'etto' is approximately 4 ounces (100 grammes). Therefore check menu carefully before ordering. Example: Scampi 2,000 lire per etto (*not* per portion).

Vegetarian

Almanacco Via Delle Route
Go early. Closed Sundays.   £

Light Meals

Break Via delle Terme
Try their 'crostoni'. Open till midnight. Closed
Sundays.   £

Le Belle Donne Via delle Belle Donne
Good home-made food. Closed Sundays.   £

3.8 *Nightlife in Florence*

Take to the Streets!

A favourite pastime is strolling around the streets, enjoying the evening air and stopping for a drink, an ice cream, a meal or a chat.

See Florence by Night

Take a bus up to Piazza Michelangelo, and see the lit-up city below: a relaxing way to spend part of an evening.

Dancing the Night Away . . .

Although Florence is not one of the world's great nightlife centres, the city has some 20 discotheques and dance halls, plus a few open-air dancing venues during summer around the Viale Michelangelo and Fiesole. They're mostly on the expensive side, so ask your local tour operator representative for advice.

Classical Music

If you're in Florence during May or June, check on opera, ballet and concert programmes of the festival called Maggio Musicale Fiorentino. October and November is the main season for concerts at the Teatro Comunale (Corso Italia 16), with an opera season that usually runs from mid-December to mid-January.

3.9 *Sunday in Florence*

There's plenty doing in Florence on a Sunday. But if you're at a loose end, here are some suggestions:

Excursions

Why not sit back, and take a trip? Excursions available on a Sunday include (a) the City Tour, (b) half-day to Pisa, or (c) a full day to Siena. See the 'Take a Trip' section for details of Pisa and Siena. Your tour operator Representative can make the reservation, or suggest other alternatives.

Shops & Markets

Shops are closed, but the Flea Market on Piazza dei Ciompi is in full swing.

Museums & Galleries

Most of the museums and galleries are open on Sundays – at least until lunchtime. Some charge a reduced entrance fee. See 'Museums & Galleries' section for further details.

Church Services

Mass in English is held at Santa Maria del Fiore (Duomo) every Saturday at 17 hrs.

Confession is held before Mass on Wednesday, Friday, Saturday 10-12 hrs; and at the Church of the Hospital of St John of God, Via Borgo Ognissanti, every Sunday and Feast Day at 10 hrs.

Your representative can provide you with full details of other services in English.

3.10 At Your Service in Florence

Banks & Exchange Bureaux
Credit Cards
American Express, Diners' Club, Visa and Access are accepted in many shops and restaurants. The following banks accept major credit cards:

Banca d'America e d'Italia,
Via Strozzi (near Piazza della Repubblica)   Tel: 27 81 11
and at Via Por Santa Maria
Cassa di Risparmio di Firenze, Via Maurizio Bufalini 4/6
Tel: 27 80 1

Credito Italiano   Via dei Vecchietti II   Tel: 27 97
Open: Monday-Thursday 8.20-13.20 and 14.45-15.45 hrs; Fridays 8.20-13.20 and 14.30-15.30 hrs. Closed on Saturdays and Sundays.

Exchange Bureau open late
Intertravel   Via dei Lamberti 39/41r
Open: Monday-Saturday 9-18.30 hrs, year-round.
Remember to take your passport. They will also cash personal cheques, if backed by a Cheque Card. There is a limit of £50.

Post Office & Telephone

Main Post Offices:
Central Post Office   Via Pietrapiana   Tel: 53155
Open: 9-13 hrs.

Post Office   Via Pellicceria   Tel: 218159
Open: 8.15-19.30 hrs. for letters, packages and telegrams.
   This Post Office is also open for telephone calls 24 hours a day, seven days a week. Use the bell outside the main entrance if the doors are shut.
   At the Railway Station, the S.I.P. Telephone Office is open 7.30-21.30 hrs. daily.

International Phone Calls
International Telephone Offices are located at Via Cavour 21 (Centro Telefonici Pubblici S.I.P.) and at the Post Offices in Via Pellicceria, Via Pietrapiana and at the Railway Station.

Emergency Phones

Police, Ambulance or Fire	113
Fire Brigade	222222
Medical (Holidays, Night – doctor on call)	477891
Ambulance, First Aid	212222

Useful Telephone Numbers and Addresses

Lost Property

Stolen Passports & Money
Should be reported to the Carabinieri (police HQ) at Borgo Ognissanti 48. A police report, made within 24 hours of the loss, is necessary for any insurance reclaim.

City Council Lost Property Office
Via Circondaria 19

Losses on Trains
Lost Property Office inside central railway station, by platform 1.

Consulates

British – Lungarno Corsini 2   Tel: 284133

US – Lungarno Amerigo Vespucci 38   Tel: 298276
Australia, Canada and Eire do not have Consuls in Florence. In case of need, contact consulates in Rome (see section 4.10).

Chemists

English Chemist   Via Tornabuoni 97

Chemists Open 24 Hours a Day:
Communale 13 – inside the main railway station
                                                    Tel: 260897
Molteni – Via dei Calzaiuoli 7r   Tel: 263490
Taverna – Piazza San Giovanni 20r   Tel: 211343

Night Chemists (open 20.00 hrs. to 08.30 hrs.):
Codeca – Via de' Ginori 50   Tel: 270849
Pagliacci – Via della Scala 49r   Tel: 275612
San Giovanni di Dio – Borgo Ognissanti 40r
                                                    Tel: 270877

Chapter Four

Rome

4.1 Introduction

'When in Rome, do as the Romans do.'

Such as? Well, just like anywhere else, the local inhabitants eat, drink and enjoy themselves. Doing all that in Roman style is good enough formula for a holiday to remember.

But, first, what about the monuments?

Of course, for a 20th-century Roman, all the guidebook sights are just part of the normal background scenery, scattered throughout the city.

Zipping through the Borghese Gardens, a Fiat-driver takes the fast route that runs beside the towering walls of ancient Rome – as well-preserved and impressive as 2,000 years ago.

He whirls through the Pincio Gate with all the courage and driving skill of a Roman charioteer, and thence down Via Veneto to Piazza Barberini, and so across central Rome. En route, there are ancient Roman columns and ruined temples – 17th-century fountains and Renaissance churches – palaces, museums and art galleries. It's an incredibly rich cultural diet which a modern Roman absorbs over a lifetime.

The best policy for first-time visitors is to take the standard city sightseeing by coach: Colosseum, Forum, Vatican City, Pantheon and a few churches. You can then return at leisure to whatever interests you most. But you cannot possibly see everything in detail!

One of the great pleasure spots of Rome is the entire area around the Spanish Steps – a sociable gathering point for tourists and Romans alike.

If you're in Rome during May, spend an hour or two at the Spanish Steps – specially decorated top to bottom with massed flowers. That's when Romans outnumber visitors around Spanish Square. All the weekend brides go there for group photographs – entire wedding parties, one after another, to pose against a gorgeous background of azaleas. For heaven's sake, pack plenty of colour film!

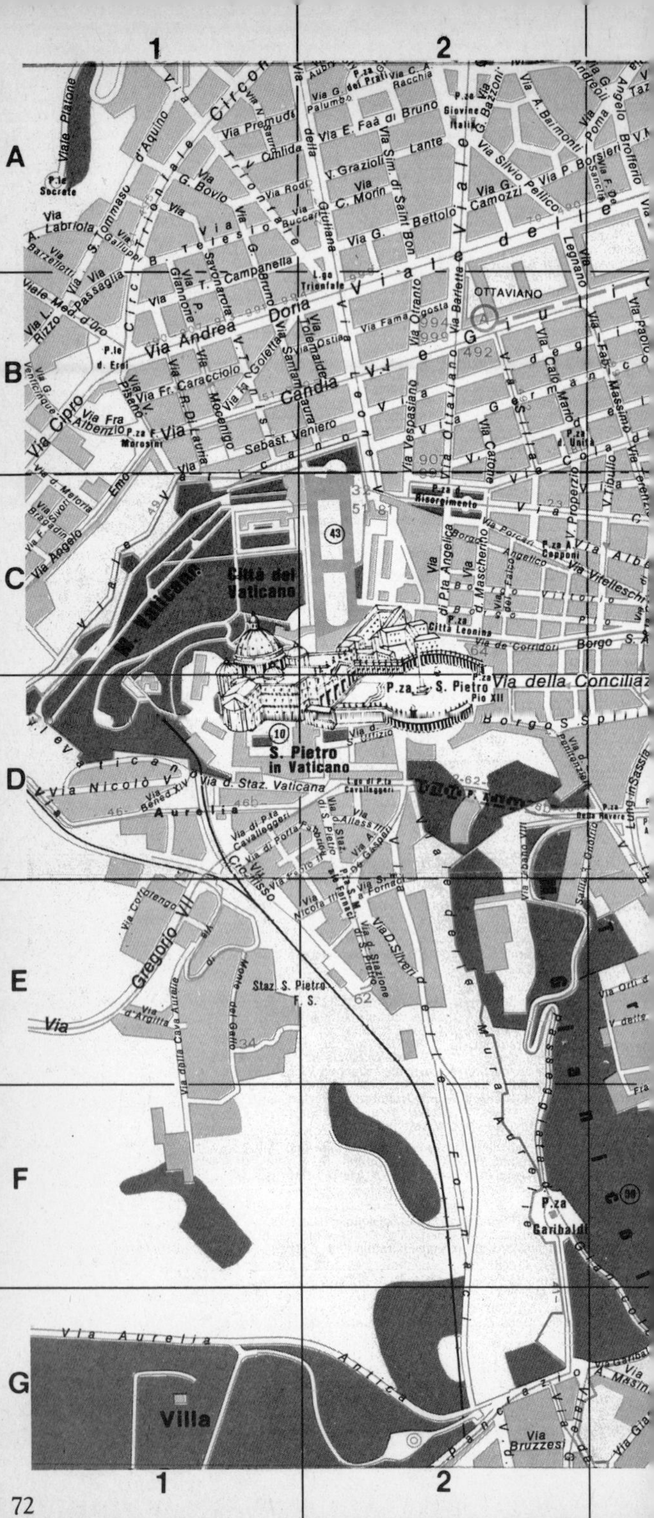

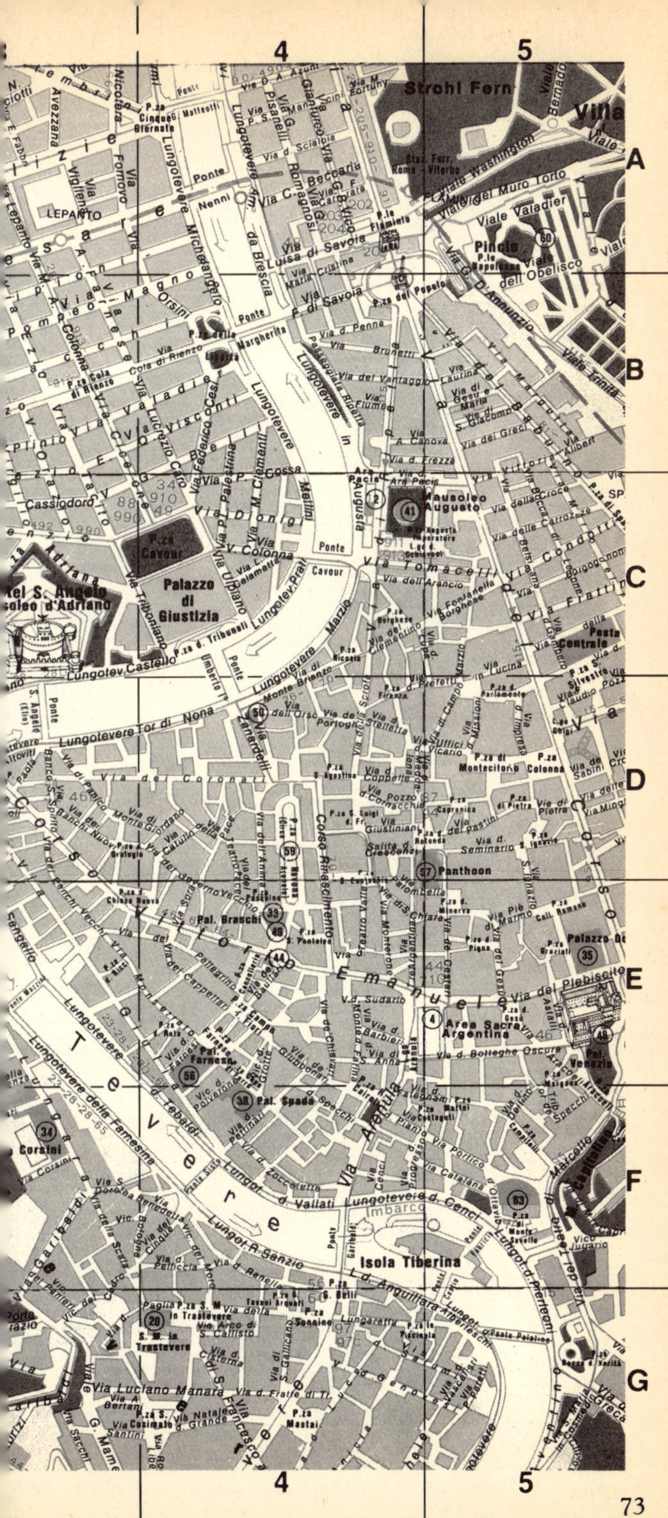

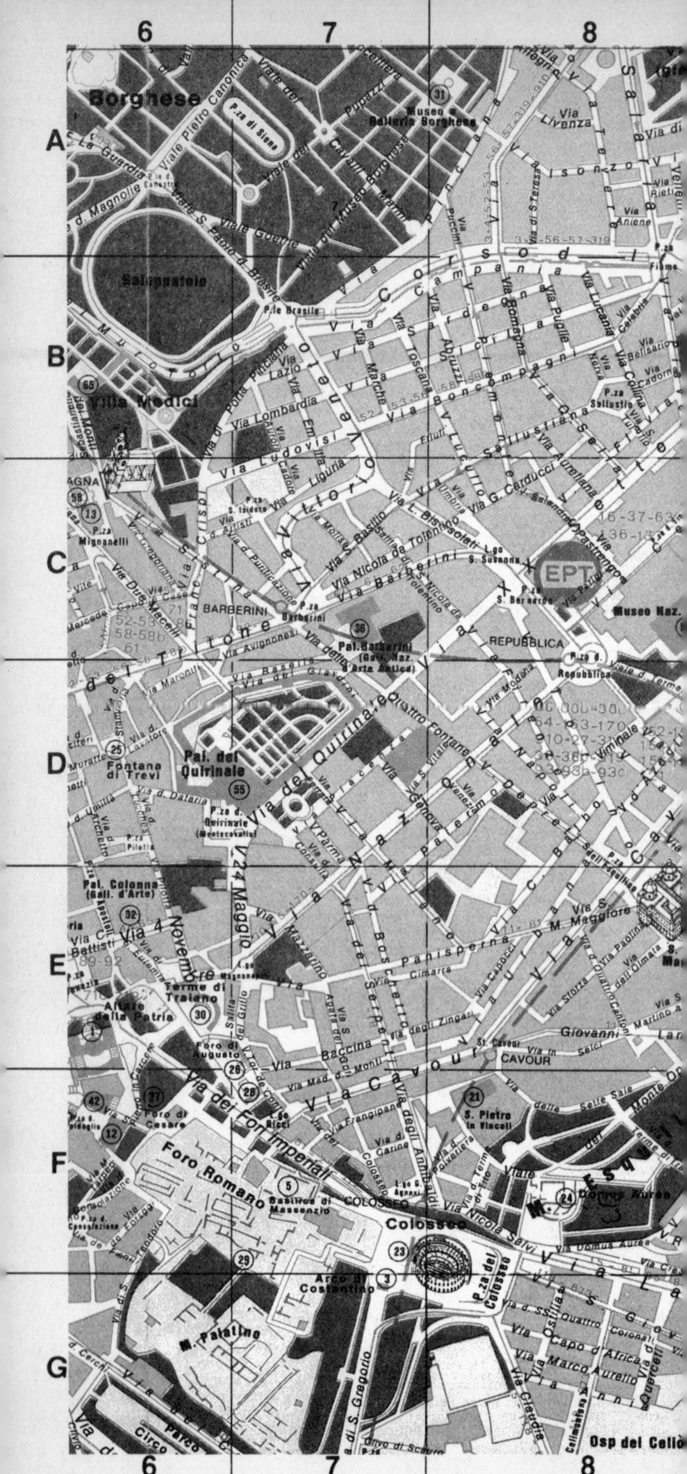

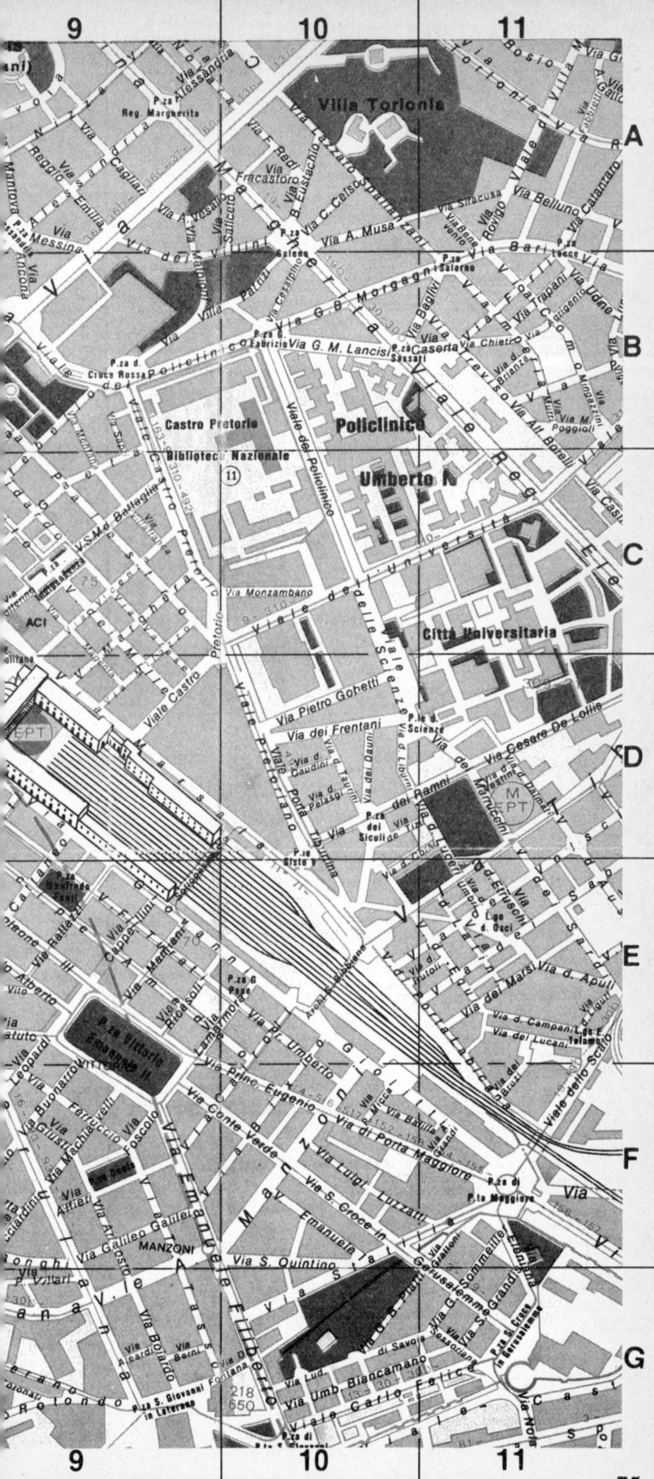

It's also a complete evening entertainment to go down to the Trevi Fountain to look at all the people, busy throwing coins into the water to ensure a return trip to Rome.

4.2 Getting Around in Rome

Rome on Foot

Central Rome still keeps a human dimension to its buildings. The little squares and piazzas ring to the sound of children, while many visitors during the season find that exploring Rome on foot is the easiest way to get around.

With two-legged tourists in mind, many street corners have signs pointing the way for walkers to reach the principal sites and locations. Because of the one-way traffic system and the non-start traffic jams, walking is often much faster than going by car but watch out for the traffic.

Public Transport

Metro

This is the fastest way of getting across Rome, unhindered by surface traffic. It's worth taking a few minutes to learn the system. However, there are only two lines. Line A – see below – can be useful in linking up several major tourist locations. Hours of operation are 06.30 to 23.30.

Tickets: Cost 700 lire, or a block of 10 for 6,000 lire.
These can be bought from:

1. Newsagents/Tabacchi with signs saying 'ATAC abbonamento bus metro'.
2. Automatic vending machines in Metro stations. Make sure you have plenty of coins with you!
3. Counters in Termini, Lepanto and Ottaviano stations.
Combined day tickets called 'Big' for Metro and buses cost 2,800 lire. These can be purchased from ATAC kiosks situated at bus terminals, or from ticket counters in the above mentioned Metro stations.

Using the System

The two lines cross handily at Termini Station:

Line A – from Via Ottaviano (near Vatican City), Flaminio (Piazza del Popolo), Piazza di Spagna and Piazza Barberini to Termini Station and thence to Cinecittà and Anagnina.

Line B – from Termini Station via Colosseum, Massimo (for Circus Maximus and Caracalla Baths), to San Paulo fuori le Mura and thence to EUR.

Metro entrances are marked with a red M. One ticket takes you anywhere on Line A or B. Entry to platforms is via automatic barriers. Work out which way to go (only a choice of two!) by reading the direction lists on the platform, showing the subsequent stops.

Doors open automatically. If the Metro is crowded, stay close to the doors. To wriggle your way out, say 'Permesso'. Most important: BEWARE OF PICKPOCKETS.

Buses

Hours of operation: 5 a.m. until midnight, but some buses only run 9-21 hrs. There are also very limited night services – 'servizio notturna' – but they do generally run as advertised.

Tickets: Cost 800 lire for 1½ hrs. or 1,000 lire for 4 hours. These are available from newspaper stands or tobacconists that display the white sign saying ATAC, with picture of a bus or from Vendita Biglietti kiosks at bus terminals. Best buy is the one-day 'Big' ticket – details in Metro section above. For longer-stay visitors, consider the weekly pass costing 11,000 lire – available only from the ATAC sales kiosk in front of Termini Station.

Using the System

Bus stops are green and called FERMATA. If the word RICHIESTA appears on the bus-stop sign, this means 'request' and you must raise your arm to halt the bus. If in doubt, put your arm out anyway! There's a list of stops under each bus number. While waiting, always check to see whether it says FERIALE as this means they run only on working days. So, if it's Sunday, you'll have to wait until Monday to catch it!

When boarding, punch your ticket in the machine at the back of the bus. Board only at the back, and exit from the middle. If the bus is crowded, then start moving towards the middle door a couple of stops before you need to alight, saying 'Permesso' as you edge through. Ring bell to stop the bus. Sorry to repeat ourselves, but don't give pickpockets a chance.

Taxis

Official taxis are yellow and should always have a working meter. If not, get out! The driver may then find that the meter is properly working, after all. There are many stands throughout the city. Here's where to find some of them:

Top of Via Veneto
In front of Termini Station
In front of St Peter's Square
Bottom of Spanish Steps
Generally in many main piazzas and tourist sites.

There are usually supplements payable on all taxi rides at night and at weekends, and for suitcases.

A normal tip is 10%.

If a taxi is called for you from the hotel or a restaurant, the meter starts working from when the driver is called. It is quite difficult to get a taxi by hailing in the street, as empty cabs are often on a call.

N.B. If you have any doubts about your taxi, note down the licence number. Avoid using drivers who approach you, as they are usually unofficial, with no meters, and can scalp you on fares.

4.3 Basic Rome

Give yourself a year, and you can see everything in Rome. Otherwise, on a short city break, at least try to cover the essentials:

(1) A morning at Vatican City and ending (if it's Sunday and the Pope's in town) with a Papal blessing at noon.
(2) Relax and enjoy the sight of other tourists at the Spanish Steps.
(3) From the Spanish Steps, explore Via Condotti and the surrounding luxury-shopping area, to gasp at the prices.
(4) Pay homage to Ancient Rome: Capitoline Hill, Roman and Imperial Forums and Colosseum.
(5) Stroll from the Pantheon to take-it-easy Piazza Navona, absorbing the atmosphere.
(6) Dine at a street restaurant in the Trastevere district.
(7) Tour the illuminations, by horse-carriage or motor coach.
(8) Cool off at the fountains of Villa d'Este, at Tivoli, 20 miles east of Rome.
(9) Enjoy a night at the opera: Teatro dell'Opera from December to June; Caracalla Baths July to mid-August.
(10) With another day to spare, dash off on the long but rewarding excursion to Naples, Pompeii and perhaps Sorrento.

Vatican City

Cross the line of white stones into St Peter's Square and you leave Italy, to enter the completely independent Vatican State. This comprises Vatican City itself – St Peter's, the Vatican palace, museums and gardens, enclosed by fortress walls – and some scattered properties such as four basilicas, several seminaries, and the Pope's summertime residence at Castel Gandolfo in the Alban Hills southeast of Rome.

Within the Vatican State's 109 acres are the Papal administrative offices, a radio station broadcasting in around 30 languages, editorial offices for varied periodicals and a daily Italian-language newspaper *L'Osservatore Romano*, a railway station and a postal service. Vatican postage stamps are valid for correspondence posted throughout Rome. If you want a Vatican postmark, buy stamps at the Post Office (left side of St Peter's Square) and drop your letters or cards into the Vatican City's blue postboxes.

About 1,000 people live in Vatican City, including 90 members of the Swiss Guard, dressed in traditional colours of the Medici Popes – yellow, red and blue. Few of the Rome-based cardinals and bishops live within the Vatican City walls, but they have the right to Vatican passports.

Best view of St Peter's is from the broad approach-road called Via della Conciliazione, enabling one to appreciate the majestic dome, designed by Michelangelo. On St Peter's Square, you cannot see the full grandeur of the dome, which reveals its full glory only from a distance.

St Peter's Square

An elliptical-shaped piazza designed by Bernini in mid-17th century, enclosed by a great colonnade. When the Pope is in residence, he appears on his balcony (top floor, second window from right) at 12 noon Sunday and pronounces a Papal blessing on the crowds gathered around the Egyptian obelisk in the Piazza below. Greatest of these occasions is on Easter Sunday when a million worshippers crowd the Square for the traditional Easter blessing – 'Urbi et Orbi' – to the City and the World.

St Peter's

Open: April–September 7-18 hrs; October–March 7-17 hrs.

To enter St Peter's – and many other churches in Rome – you should be soberly dressed: no shorts; no above-the-knee skirts; no sleeveless dresses (though women can get by with a scarf draped over shoulders). Otherwise you will be politely turned away.

First built as a shrine in 324 AD for the mortal remains of St Peter, the Basilica was rebuilt over a thousand years later. Various architects and artists worked on the building, including Bramante, Raphael, Michelangelo and Peruzzi. Finally completed in the shape of a Latin Cross, St Peter's was consecrated in 1626.

Immediately right after you enter is Michelangelo's most famous work, the Pietà, sculpted when he was 25 years old, already at the height of his creative genius. The masterpiece has been protected by bulletproof glass ever since 1972 when a crazed Hungarian attacked the sculpture with a hammer.

On the floor of the central nave are marked the lengths of other well-known cathedrals. All are dwarfed by St Peter's, though St Paul's, London, falls short by only six feet.

On the right, as you approach the Papal altar, is a bronze statue of St Peter, whose right foot is now worn smooth after being kissed by millions of pilgrims ever since the 13th century.

The Papal altar was designed by Bernini, and is known as the Baldacchino (a baldaquin or canopy). Bees carved on the columns are the family emblem of the Barbarini family, to which Pope Urban VIII belonged when he unveiled the canopy in 1633. In front of the altar, on a lower level, is the reputed tomb of St Peter, centred beneath the awe-inspiring dome.

To appreciate Michelangelo's dome, what better way than by climbing to the top! This is possible every day from 8 a.m. until one hour before the Basilica closes. At the left of the Basilica is entrance to the lift which carries you up to the 18-ft-high statues that overlook the square – a good viewpoint for photographs and a cup of coffee. The top of the dome is then accessible by climbing some 300 stairs up a narrow spiral. If you can make it to the exterior gallery, the reward is a spectacular view right across Rome.

Papal Audience

With a letter from your priest, it is possible to get admission tickets by applying at the Prefectura's office which is open Monday and Tuesday mornings. General Papal audiences take place Wednesday mornings from 10.00-12.00 when the Pope is in Rome.

Vatican Treasury

Inside St Peter's
A modern, well displayed museum giving a chance to see many treasures and past glories: chalices, crosses, vestments and early Christian relics.

Vatican Museums

Entrance in Viale Vaticano, price 8,000 lire. The museums are open Monday-Saturday 9-14 hrs. At Easter, and July to September, they are open 9-17 hrs. The last Sunday of each month (if not Easter Sunday) the museums are open from 9-14, and entrance is free. All are closed on religious holidays.

The Vatican collections are housed in approximately 1,000 rooms and corridors. Needless to say, it would take a lifetime to see everything in detail! Short-stay visitors normally skim through in 90 minutes, with a short pause at selected highlights. Devotees should assign at least a whole day, perhaps following a recommended routing that takes 5 hours to complete. There's a snack bar, for restoring the exhausted.

If you want a compromise between those two extremes, it's worth taking an organised tour with a guide who can bring those highlights vividly to life. For guide-yourself visitors, headphones can be rented for the Sistine Chapel and the Raphael Rooms. Remember to have 100- or 200-lire coins handy.

At the entrance, which is a 15-minute walk round from St Peter's, you take a lift to an upper floor and work down to ground level. Routing is on a one-way system, so you cannot backtrack; but there is a colour-coded choice of four different routes including an Egyptian Museum, the Pio Clementino Museum of Greek and Roman antiquities, varied galleries and of course the Sistine Chapel. Some routes pause for the Vatican Library, containing many treasures including love letters from Henry VIII to Anne Boleyn.

Sistine Chapel

The Sistine Chapel, named after Pope Sixtus IV, is the Pope's private chapel where the cardinals meet when it's the occasion to elect a new pope. Built at the end of the 15th century, it was decorated by some of history's greatest painters. The chapel is best known for the contribution of Michelangelo. Commissioned to paint the ceiling in 1508 by Pope Julius II, he completed it within four years, working single-handed while lying on his back. Some twenty years later he was asked to paint the altar wall: *The Last Judgement*, regarded as one of the greatest masterpieces of Renaissance art.

Currently that work is undergoing on-the-spot restoration, financed by a $3 million gift from a Japanese TV company in exchange for all filming, book and photographic rights until beginning of the 21st century.

The immense task began in 1984 with restoration of Michelangelo's ceiling paintings – dedicated work by three Italian specialists who employed the same historic design of scaffolding used by Michelangelo himself. The ceiling portrays the main events from the Book of Genesis: God separates light and darkness; creates sun, moon and plant life; divides land and sea; creates Adam and Eve; then the Fall, and Expulsion from Eden; Noah's Sacrifice, followed by the Flood, and Noah's Drunkenness. Results of the ceiling restoration have been truly magnificent, revealing every detail in the original brilliance of colour. Luminosity has been restored to scenes that had been darkened by centuries of candle smoke. Judge for yourself. Take binoculars or opera glasses, to intensify your enjoyment.

Current restoration of *The Last Judgement* will hopefully be completed by 1992. While the work is in progress, the altar wall will remain hidden from the public. In its place, a false wall with a Kodak reproduction of the original will have to satisfy the millions of visitors.

Vatican Picture Gallery – the Pinacoteca

Here there are yet more treasures by Giotto, Raphael,

Titian and Leonardo de Vinci; and the 'Coronation of the Virgin' by two artists who often completed works begun by Raphael.

Museo Storico – Historical Museum

This contains carriages, arms, uniforms and relics of the disbanded Papal armies.

Vatican Gardens

Visits to these beautifully kept gardens are on the following weekdays:

March to October –
    Thursday   Tours of gardens
    Tuesday and Friday   Tours of gardens and Basilica
    Monday and Saturday Tours of gardens and Sistine
                                              Chapel

November to February –
    Tuesday, Thursday and Saturday   Tours of gardens

All these visits leave from the Information Office at 10 a.m. This office is at the left-hand side of St Peter's Square, near the Arco delle Campane (the Bell Arch).

Spanish Steps

Much of the tourist colour of Rome is supplied by the visitors themselves. At the Spanish Steps, tourists by the thousand, dressed in all kinds of gear, provide a huge source of entertainment to the local Roman youth. At the end of April and beginning of May the Steps are covered in massed flowers. Then, at least until October, the Spanish Steps are covered in tourists, even more colourful than the May azaleas.

It's like a setting for open-air opera, with a large and brilliant chorus ready to break out any moment into song, dance or drama. Young backpackers sit writing letters home. Others just sit, waiting for something to happen, and meanwhile enjoying the passing scene.

Occasional groups burst into song, especially if someone has brought a guitar. Tourists take photos of artists' drawing caricatures of tourists taking photographs. Some of the more decorative off-duty soldiers of the Italian Army parade their uniforms in front of female tourists, and look eager.

To the tinkle of horse-bells, carriages wait hopefully in the Piazza di Spagna for the perfect tourist who may take a 50-minute ride without asking the price first.

Altogether, it's a fun place to visit. The sightseeing rationale is the splendid view over to St Peter's, seen from the top terrace where the church of Trinità dei Monti dominates the skyline. Bottom, left, is the Keats–Shelley House. The boat-shaped fountain in the square was designed by Bernini's father, Pietro. The sculpture of a stranded boat, leaking badly, is called 'Fontana della Barcaccia' and is used by many sightseers to bathe their aching feet.

Ancient Rome

The simplest way to get a general introduction to the splendours of ancient Rome is to take the standard coach tour. The great highlights are the Roman and Imperial Forums, Colosseum, Palatine Hill, the Circus Maximus, Caracalla Baths and much more. Even on a 3-hour tour, you are still only touching the surface. But at least you'll then have a general idea of the layout, for supplementary sightseeing.

See the Piazza Venezia, the Victor Emmanuel Monument (the white wedding-cake which most Romans regard as a dazzling eyesore), and the Piazza del Campidoglio. Stop to visit the Capitoline Museums if you want to see a great collection of Greek and Roman sculptures. Otherwise, continue to the splendid viewpoint over ancient Rome, behind the Palazzo Senatoria.

Below are the three columns of the Temple of Vespasian, and the Arch of Septimus Severus. Take the flight of steps down (left of the Palazzo Senatorio) to reach the entrance to the Mamertine Prison – St Peter's old gaol – in the northwest corner of the Forum.

From there is a choice of several routings. You could work northwards to peek over the railings around Caesar's Forum and then continue across the broad Via Dei Fori Imperiali particularly to inspect Trajan's Forum, which includes Trajan's Column and the Market (see next section). Alternatively you could tour the Roman Forum itself, moving towards the Palatine Hill.

On either routing, you could end up at the Colosseum.

Colosseum

Metro: Colosseo
One of Rome's most impressive buildings, inaugurated 80 AD by Emperor Titus. Over 50,000 spectators seated in 3 tiers were able to watch gladiator fights, mock sea battles and the baiting and killing of wild beasts. The upper tiers have been well restored, and there is plenty to see. Even the animal pens still exist, under the main floor. Most impressive are the enormous corridors through which thousands of spectators poured out after the show, emptying the Colosseum in ten minutes.
Open: 09.00 to one hour before sunset (latest being 19.00 hrs.).
Entrance fee, 3,000 lire, only for upper levels.

Trevi Fountain

The Trevi Fountain starred in the movie *Three Coins in the*

Fountain, and has never since lacked publicity. It's one of the liveliest corners of Rome, with souvenir vendors, stalls selling hot pizza, hundreds of tourists throwing coins into the fountain, or posing for cameras against the Trevi background.

An average $300 a day is cast into the spectacular cascade of water and marble, under the benevolent gaze of Neptune with a supporting cast of Salubrity and Abundance, four statues that depict the seasons, and tritons riding sea-horses. Who goes fishing? The coinage harvest is devoted to charities, including the International Red Cross. A private enterprise team started cleaning up at night: they ended in gaol instead.

Piazza Navona

A very charming and popular square, especially in the evening, full of people selling paintings, sketches and jewellery. After a hard day's sightseeing, here's a great place to rest your feet. In ancient times, the area was covered by a large stadium or circus built by Domitian (81-96 AD) - hence the elliptical shape. After falling into disuse, the area was revived in the 15th century, and remains one of the most delightful pedestrian areas in Rome. If you're in Rome during the Christmas/New Year period, visit the Piazza for its traditional Christmas Market running from 15 December to 6 January.

Particularly the Piazza Navona is known for its fountains:

La Fontana dei Quattro Fiumi
The Fountain of Four Rivers, designed by Gian Lorenzo Bernini and representing the Ganges, Nile, Danube and Plate Rivers. Magnificent!

Fontana del Moro
Fountain of the Moor. The fountain was built in late 16th century. The main character, the Moor, was designed by Bernini in 1653 when he was commissioned to renovate the monument.

Fontana di Nettuno
Neptune's Fountain was likewise constructed in 16th century, but Neptune and the surrounding figures were not installed until the 19th century.

4.4 Other Sights in Rome

The amount of Roman sightseeing and historic interest is quite fantastic: ancient columns and ruined temples - 17th-century fountains and Renaissance churches - great palaces, museums and art galleries. Outside the immense city walls are the ruined aqueducts, with their piers striding down across the open countryside towards Rome, whence they brought all the water supplies for the ancient Imperial capital.

There is delight in following through the march of the centuries: noting the great pagan temples of the Roman Forum; conjuring up the wild and brutal Roman holidays in the Colosseum; visiting the Caracalla Baths – one of the most grandiose buildings of 3rd-century Rome; exploring Catacombs that played a big part in early Christian history; noting the blank spots – the Dark Ages when the barbarians took over; and then seeing the great triumph of the Renaissance, when men created new expressions of faith and worship.

Amid this embarrassment of sightseeing riches, don't panic that you're going to miss something. Just pick out the highlights which could interest you most, and leave the rest till next time.

Monuments

Today, much of Rome is kept under wraps.

The stone most commonly used in Rome is travertine. The name derives from its place of origin – Tivoli, Latin name *tiburtina*, which lies in the hills east of Rome. Travertine is a white limestone which the Romans employed for their most grandiose buildings, from majestic temples to the Colosseum. These same rocks were quarried for the greatest buildings of the Christian period and of the modern age.

The various kinds of tufo or 'cappellaccio' are related to travertine, but are less resistant and much less attractive. Buildings in travertine, like those in baked clay brick, were often finished with a plaster called 'pozzolana' which was dug near Rome. This plaster, still much used, gives buildings in Rome their characteristic purplish red colour.

Aurelian Walls

A 12-mile ring of fortifications around the city, built during the reign of Emperor Aurelian (270–275 AD). Much of the wall still exists, in good condition. Several of the original 18 main gates provide good vantage points from which to view the city, including Porta Pia (renovated by Michelangelo), Porta San Sebastiano and Porta San Paolo.

Augustus' Altar of Peace

Lungotevere in Augusta

A reconstruction of a monumental altar erected by Augustus in 13 BC to celebrate the establishment of peace throughout the Roman lands, and the end of 20 years of civil war.

Open: Winter – Saturday 9-14 hrs; Sunday 9-13 hrs;
Summer – Tuesday, Thursday and Saturday 9-14 & 16-19 hrs; Sunday 9-13 hrs.

Castel Sant' Angelo
Lungotevere di Castello
Originally intended as Hadrian's mausoleum, it was built around 135 AD. In 271 AD it was remodelled as a fort by Aurelian, when he was building the circle of city walls. In middle ages the castle became the Papal stronghold and prison. Inside there is a Papal suite and a military museum. The terrace gives an excellent panorama of St Peter's and the city of Rome. The bronze angel perched on the castle pinnacle recalls a legend dating from about 600 AD, when plague was devastating the city. Pope Gregory the Great (590–604) ordered a procession – after which he had a vision of an angel re-sheathing its sword.
Open: Tuesday-Saturday 9-13 hrs; Sunday 9-12 hrs. Monday closed.
Entrance: 3,000 lire.

Circo Massimo (Circus Maximus)
Metro: Circus Maximus
The Great Circus – former scene of the Ben Hur type of chariot races – was built around 2nd century BC. In its heyday, the Circus could hold 300,000 spectators. Successive emperors lavished funds on improvements and extensions. In the middle you can still see where the number of laps were recorded by the moving of 7 large wooden eggs on the central Spina, or dividing barrier. The circus fell into disuse after the fall of Rome.
Open daily. No entrance fee.

Fori Imperiali
Via dei Fori Imperiali
Rome outgrew the main Forum, so additions were made just north of the Foro Romano, along the line of Mussolini's Imperial Fora Way which leads from Piazza Venezia direct to the Colosseum. These extensions gave Emperors a status-symbol chance to vie with their predecessors, by trying to build the most imposing addition. Judge for yourself. In date order, the contestants are:

Caesar's Forum
Here you can see the remains of a temple of Venus, and the site of the Mamertine Prison at the foot of the Capitoline Hill, where tradition says that St Peter was jailed. The prison is now a chapel called San Pietro in Carcere (St Peter in prison), giving access to the gloomy dungeons where enemies of Rome were incarcerated. Christian martyrs are listed at the entrance.

Augustus's Forum
Built to commemorate Augustus's victory in 42 BC at Philippi, where he avenged the death of Caesar (his

adopted father) by the slaying of Cassius and Brutus. Still standing are three columns of the Temple of Mars Ultor – Mars the Avenger. Some other Corinthian colums also remain.

Nerva's Forum

Regrettably, about all that remains are two Corinthian columns and the base of the Temple of Minerva.

Trajan's Forum

Posterity has given top rating to Trajan's Forum, inaugurated in 113 AD. Most remarkable is Trajan's Column, which celebrated his victory over the Dacians (inhabitants of modern-day Romania). A spiral frieze with over 100 scenes and 2,500 figures winds its way up the 125-ft column. It forms a complete record of the campaign, depicting uniforms, weapons, siege operations and military techniques in faithful detail. It's like a Bayeaux Tapestry in marble, unrolling the story in sequence from bottom to top, originally in full colour that has long since faded. Aloft, a bronze statue of Trajan was exchanged in 1587 for the present statue of St Peter.

The site also has the remains of the 6-storey shopping centre; fruit and flowers on ground floor; oil and wine on the 2nd; pepper and spices on 3rd and 4th; social services on the fifth; fish tanks fed by fresh- and salt-water aqueducts at roof level.

Pantheon – Piazza della Rotonda

A 'must' to visit. The Pantheon was reconstructed by Hadrian in 125 AD and converted into a church in the 7th century by Pope Boniface IV. You enter through the original Roman bronze doors. Within, the fantastic dome is still precisely as designed in Hadrian's time, with sunshine (or rain) pouring through a central opening called an oculus. Elements of the design have inspired innumerable architects over the centuries. It's pleasant to study the architecture from one of the bars facing the entrance.
Open: Tuesday-Saturday 9-14 hrs; Sunday 9-13 hrs. Mondays closed. No entrance fee.

Catacombs

Catacombs? There are many to explore. If time is limited, choose the Catacombs of S. Agnese, which are close to the centre of Rome on the Via Nomentana. Otherwise, if time is not so pressing, go out along the Appian Way – so rich in early Christian history. A pilgrimage through the long burial chambers is one of the memorable experiences of a lifetime. The simplest tombs were dug and shaped into cubicles or crypts to hold sarcophagi. Among the best known are:

Catacombe di San Sebastiano
Via Appia Antica 132 (beneath the church of San Sebastiano)
This is prime choice. Three mausoleums with stucco decorations date from the 1st century. It is believed that the bodies of Saints Peter and Paul were concealed here until their permanent basilicas were built.
Open: Daily 8.30-12.00 hrs; 14.30-17.00 hrs. Closed Thursdays.
Entrance 2,000-3,000 lire.

Catacombe di San Callisto
Via Appia Antica 110 – just along the road from San Sebastiano.
Built on four levels, extending several kilometres. Dates from 2nd century. See the 3rd, 7th and 8th century frescoes. Also the 3rd century crypt of the popes.
Open: Daily 8.30-12.00 hrs; 14.30-17.00 hrs. Closed Wednesdays.
Entrance: 2,000-3,000 lire.

Catacombe di Priscilla
Via Salaria 430
Located on the northern side of Rome, these catacombs contain 2nd century frescoes. Amongst them is the oldest known image of the Madonna and Child.
Open: Tuesday-Sunday 8.30-12.00 hrs; 14.30-17 hrs. Closed Mondays.
Entrance: 2,000-3,000 lire.

Churches

Rome is a city of 300 churches, of which 80 are dedicated to the Virgin Mary.

St Mary Major (Santa Maria Maggiore)
Metro: Cavour or Termini
This basilica is the largest of the churches dedicated to Mary. Built by Pope Sixtus III (432–440), it contains some 36 panels of beautiful mosaics. The Old Testament scenes are well worth studying. At the end of the nave, a triumphal arch is decorated with scenes of the Annunciation, and the childhood of Christ including Our Lady. Other treasures include the Pauline Chapel.
Open: 7-19 hrs.

St. Laurence outside the Walls (San Lorenzo fuori le Mura)
Piazzale del Verano
An intriguing church, originally the site of a chapel built in the 4th century by Constantine the Great over the tomb of St Lawrence, martyred by being grilled over a gridiron. By

the Middle Ages two churches had been built back to back, which were later joined to form one. If you ask at the Sacristy, you may be able to see the 12th century double cloisters. A tip is in order here.
Open: April-September 9.00-18.30 hrs; October-March 9.00-14.30 hrs.

St John Lateran (San Giovanni in Laterano)
Metro: San Giovanni (Line A)
Built during the reign of Constantine the Great, St John Lateran was the cathedral of Rome for about 1,000 years.

The central bronze gate with its two porticos came from the ancient Curia in the Forum. There are many beautiful mosaics to see, and a restored fresco by Giotto in the middle nave.

The basilica is perhaps best known for its 'Scala Santa' – Holy Staircase. According to tradition, the 28 marble stairs were originally in Pilate's residence in Jerusalem, and were used by Christ during his trial. The steps are still climbed by pilgrims on their knees.
Open: 7 a.m. to ½ hour before sunset. Some parts are closed 12.30-15.30 hrs.

Museums & Galleries

Rome offers four types of Museums: – State – Municipal – Vatican – Private.

The state museums, galleries and monuments can usually be visited free of charge on the first and third Saturday, and on the second and fourth Sunday of the month.

Municipal museums and galleries (for example, Capitoline and Barracco Museums) and the Vatican Museums are free on the last Sunday of the month.

Times of opening are like an Italian's temper – liable to change at a moment's notice! So be prepared. Staff problems or renovations can disrupt opening times, or close off entire sections of great museums, sometimes for years on end. Before making a special journey across Rome, check the current opening hours.
Entrance fees range from about 2,000 to 5,000 lire. Also liable to change!

Capitoline Museums – Musei Capitolini
Piazza dei Campidoglio (near Piazza Venezia)
Tel: 6782862
The twin-palace Capitoline Museums house Europe's oldest public art collection, founded 1471 by Pope Sixtus IV who needed space for his accumulation of Greek and Roman sculptures. The majestic Piazza itself was designed by Michelangelo in 1538, but was not completed until a hundred years later.

The location is among the most historic in Rome: should be visited, even if you skip the museums. Built on the lowest of Rome's seven hills – the Capitoline Hill – the site has been the centre of its city government since ancient times. Here Brutus spoke, after the death of Julius Caesar. Formerly, a splendid bronze statue of Marcus Aurelius stood in the centre of the square; but atmospheric pollution was eating away the Emperor and his steed, who are now stabled elsewhere.

On the southern summit of the Capitoline stood the magnificent Temple of Jupiter, the remains of which can be seen in the Palazzo dei Conservatori. On the northern peak was the Temple of Juno Moneta, later occupied by the Roman mint, and now the site of the church of Santa Maria d'Aracoeli.

Open: Tuesday and Thursday 9-14 hrs; 17-20 hrs; Wednesday and Friday 9-14 hrs; Saturday 9-14 hrs; 20.30-23.00 hrs; Sunday 9.00-12.30 hrs; Monday closed.

Roman Civilization Museum – Museo della Civiltà Romana

Piazza G. Agnelli   Tel: 5926138
Metro – Line B to EUR – Stop: Fermi
Special for history buffs: reproductions which document Roman history, and the expansion of the Empire. Of particular interest is the scale model of ancient Rome. This museum was built by the Fiat Company, and donated to the city.
Open: Tuesday and Thursday 9-17 hrs; Wednesday, Friday and Saturday 9-14 hrs; Sunday 9-13 hrs. Monday closed.

Etruscan Museum – Museo Nationale de Villa Giulia

Piazzale di Villa Giulia, in the north-west corner of Borghese Gardens   Tel: 3601951
Built as a villa in mid-16th century by pleasure-loving Pope Julius III, this magnificent Renaissance building contains the world's finest collection of Etruscan art and artifacts from pre-Roman civilisation. Highlights include a recumbent 'Bride and Bridegroom' in terracotta, from 6th century BC; the Apollo of Vejo sculpture; and innumerable finds from Etruscan cemeteries. Well laid out.
Open: Tuesday-Saturday 9-19 hrs; Sunday 9-13 hrs; Monday closed.

Museo di Palazzo Venezia

Piazza Venezia   Tel: 6798865
Splendidly located at Rome's busiest traffic intersection, the Venezia Palace was built mid-15th century, and later given to the Venetian Republic for use as their embassy – hence the name. The building was frequently seen on

news-reels of the 1930's, when dictator Mussolini made impassioned speeches from the central balcony to cheering crowds in the piazza below. From that balcony Mussolini declared war against Britain and France on 10 June 1940, just after Dunkirk, when he felt the time was ripe to help Hitler divide the spoils of victory.

Today the palace houses a collection of paintings, statues, tapestries and porcelains, supplemented by temporary art exhibitions. Most interesting is the Map Room (Sala del Mappamondo) – so named for its wall painting of the world as depicted in 1495. This enormous room – 70 feet by 40 – was used by Mussolini as his single-occupancy office.
Open: Tuesday-Saturday 9-14 hrs; Sunday 9-13 hrs; Monday closed.

Keats–Shelley Memorial House
Piazza di Spagna   Tel: 6784235
A little corner of England, beside the Spanish Steps: the house where Keats died in 1821, preserved as a memorial to the Romantic poets. The floor where Keats lived is filled to the brim with pictures, letters and mementoes of Keats, Shelley, Byron and Leigh Hunt. Everything is labelled in English as well as Italian. Just opposite is Babington's Tea Room, where you can have English tea and muffins.
Open: Summer: Monday-Friday 9-13 hrs; 15.30-18.00 hrs; Winter: Monday-Friday 9-13 hrs; 14.30-17.00 hrs.

National Roman Museum – Nazionale Romano or Museo delle Terme
Entrance Piazza della Republica/Piazza dei Cinquecento, across the square from Termini Station
More of the glory of ancient Rome – the Baths of Diocletian, built 298 AD. It was largest of all the Roman Baths, 32 acres in area, even bigger than the Caracalla complex. The water supply was destroyed in 538 AD, and the Baths fell into disuse. Today, part of the site is devoted to the National Roman Museum which houses a great collection of Greek and Roman statues, and beautiful mosaics.

A masterpiece of 1st-century Classical art is the fresco that covered four walls from a room in the Empress Livia's villa at Prima Porta, north of Rome. Its vivid colours make it hard to believe it was painted almost 2,000 years ago!
Open: Tuesday-Saturday 9-14 hrs; Sunday 9-13 hrs; Monday closed.

Galleria Barberini (Palazzo Barberini)
Via Quattro Fontane
Metro: Barberini
A Baroque palace built by Cardinal Maffeo Barberini after he became Pope Urbain VIII. The architects were the two

top men of Baroque style – Borromini and Bernini, who worked on this spectacular Barberini family home from 1627 to 1633.

Today, the huge building is occupied partly by Italy's National Gallery, and partly by a military organisation. One of the gems of the collection is Raphael's portrait of his bosomy mistress, La Fornarina. There is also a portrait of Henry VIII by Holbein; and works by El Greco, Titian and Lippi.

The apartments of the Barberini family are worth visiting for their costumes, china and period furniture.
Open: Tuesday-Saturday 9-19 hrs; Sunday 9-13 hrs; Monday 9-14 hrs.

Galleria Borghese
Piazzale del Museo Borghese
A relatively small palace, built in 1613 for the wealthy Cardinal Scipione Borghese – Pope Paul V – who was a great collector of ancient statues. In 1803 Prince Camillo Borghese married Napoleon's sister, Pauline, and most of the original collection was shipped to the Louvre in Paris.

The present sculpture collection was formed after Camillo's death, and is displayed on the ground floor. The most renowned work is a statue of Pauline Bonaparte, carved by Canova. Pauline enjoyed a lively reputation in Rome – while her husband supervised his estates in Northern Italy – and displays herself nude, as Venus the goddess of love.

The upper floor of the Borghese Gallery has been closed lengthily for restoration, and re-opening remains vague. Some of the stored paintings are sometimes displayed at the Palazzo Venezia.
Open: Tuesday-Saturday 9-19 hrs; Sunday and Monday 9-13 hrs.

Galleria Colonna
Via della Pilotta 17
A private collection housed in the huge Palazzo Colonna (another of Rome's great families). Specials include a Veronese portrait of an unknown nobleman, a set of landscapes by Gaspare Dughet, and paintings by Tintoretto and Poussin.
Open Saturdays only, 9-13 hrs. Closed August.

Galleria Doria Pamphili
Piazza del Collegio Romano 1a
A small gallery bursting at the seams with gems, including a Velasquez portrait of Pope Innocento X, a member of the Pamphili family. Other masterpieces include works by Rubens, Filippo Lippi, Caravaggio and Breughel. An easy-to-manage gallery! It is advisable to buy the catalogue, as the pictures only have numbers on them.

The entrance fee includes the picture gallery only, and there is a supplement for the State apartments. These are a 'must'. Visitors are guided by a curator, and a tip is recommended.
Open: Tuesday, Friday, Saturday and Sunday 10-13 hrs.

Galleria Nazional d'Arte Moderna
Viale delle Belle Arti 131
The National Gallery of Modern Art features the 19th and 20th centuries, including works by Matisse, Picasso and Modigliani.
Open: Tuesday-Saturday 9.00-13.30 hrs; Sunday 9.00-12.30 hrs; Monday closed.

3.5 Take a Trip from Rome

Of course, no city break is long enough for all the sightseeing that Rome can offer. But, for a change of scene, why not take a trip out of town? There are many possibilities. But let's keep the short-list down to a choice of two all-time favourites: half-day Tivoli and Villa d'Este; or whole-day Naples, Pompeii and Sorrento.

Tivoli and Villa D'Este
For an afternoon or evening outing, the most popular trip is to the hillside village of Tivoli, where wealthy Romans built their splendid summer palaces, 19 miles east of the city. En route, as the road climbs, you pass through centuries'-old olive groves. You also pass the sulphur baths of Bagni di Tivoli, but there's no need to halt unless you get high on sulphuretted hydrogen.

At Tivoli itself, the 16th-century fountains, cascades and gardens of the Villa d'Este are the principal attraction – a cool relief during the hot summer season. The gardens are floodlit after dark from April through October. The entire 7-acre complex is refreshing and light-hearted, to comprise one of Europe's most delightful water fantasies.

See also the ruins of Hadrian's Villa – Villa Adriana – built 125–135 AD. There was nothing suburban about *this* villa! The 3-mile perimeter of the emperor's estate enclosed a mammoth building project which included an imperial palace, several baths, a couple of theatres and some libraries.

Within this idyllic summer retreat, Hadrian reproduced many ideas of art and architecture which he had acquired during lengthy travels around the Roman Empire. Some 300 items from his collection of sculptures and other objets d'art now adorn the major museums of Europe.

See Naples and Pompeii
A motorway southwards brings Naples, Pompeii and Sorrento within reach of a whole-day excursion. It's a long

trail, but very rewarding: the final stage of the old-time Grand Tour which normally ended with a sojourn in Naples and an awed visit to the smoking lip of Mount Vesuvius.

Naples? On a quick look round, you can get a good impression of the superbly beautiful Bay of Naples, especially when viewed from the up-market residential area called Vomero. Pause at Santa Lucia – the fishing harbour that launched the song – where the waterfront is lined with seafood restaurants. Otherwise, the joyous street life of central Naples is best seen from the armchair comfort of the motor coach.

Out past the industrial zone, otherwise lacking in sightseeing potential, you start getting good views of Vesuvius. Along the road is a richly fertile garden landscape, green with vineyards and lush vegetation. In that gorgeous setting, it's easy to understand why farmers have continued to work the terraced hillsides despite what happened in AD 79, when Vesuvius blew its top.

Pompeii is magnificent. Excavation continues. Every year there are more discoveries that help archaeologists reconstruct every tiny detail of daily life in the city that suddenly died 1900 years ago. Fascinating!

Some day-trips manage to include Sorrento – perched on a cliff-top, with perpendicular drop to a very narrow strip of beach. Major first-class hotels are lined along the cliff amid luxuriant gardens, dripping with flowers everywhere. Views across the Bay are idyllic.

Time for shopping? Sorrento specialises in wood and mother-of-pearl inlaid work, leather items, hand-embroidered linen, silks, cameos, coral and onyx. Many items you can buy direct from craftsmen in their side-street workshops.

4.6 *Shopping in Rome*

Directly opposite the Spanish Steps is the narrow Via Condotti, where wealthy Romans go shopping. Italian men say: 'It's heaven for ladies, but hell for husbands'.

For Italy's finest displays of jewellery, just pretend to be a millionaire and stroll through the breathtaking showrooms of Bulgari – just a few steps down Via Condotti, and considered to be one of the world's greatest jewellery shops.

Along the Via Condotti, fragrant with big names like Gucci, most of the goods displayed are not priced; or the figures are so discreet that you need binoculars to read them. If you have to know the price before deciding to buy, you can't afford it! There are shirts at £80, shoes that start at £100, while a simple trouser belt costs £40.

The parallel and side streets are likewise into the jewellery and high-fashion business. At the cheaper end of the area, shoes sink as low as £50 a pair.

To clued-up local Romans, best value shopping can be found in the Via Cola di Rienzo area, near the Vatican (metro: Ottaviano). Other middle-income citizens choose the reasonably-priced stores of Via Nazionale. Sometimes bargains can be hunted down in shops around the Trevi Fountain district. Here are some more shopping areas, and the designer labels to look for:
Via Borgognona: Gianfranco Ferre; Fendi
Via Bocca de Leone: Valentino; Trussardi Gianni Versace; Ungaro
Via del Babuino: Giorgio Armani

Department Stores

Rinascente – Piazza Colonna and Piazza Fiume
Upim – Via del Tritone
Standa – Via Cola di Rienzo 173

General Opening & Closing Hours

All shops are tightly shuttered and streets empty for lunch and siesta, from 12.30 or 13.00 hrs until 15.30 or 16.00 hrs. Then business continues until 19.30 or 20 hrs. Shops are open Monday to Saturday, mostly with Saturday afternoon closed. In winter, shops don't bother to open Monday morning.

Markets

Flea Market

Porta Portese in the Trastevere area
Open Sunday mornings
This flea market is full of atmosphere. you can buy almost anything. Always barter! Not many real bargains, but it's all good fun. Because of the crowds, be extra careful with purses and wallets.

Clothes Market

Via Sannio, to the side of Porta S. Giovanni
Open Monday-Saturday until 1 p.m.
Metro: S. Giovanni (Line A); or bus No. 4, 81, 85 or 87.
This is Rome's biggest clothing market.

Fruit, Flower & Vegetable Market

Piazzo Campo de Fiori (close to the river, a few blocks north of Ponte Sisto bridge)
Open Monday-Saturday 6 a.m. until 2 p.m.
A colourful food market, giving you a chance to learn colloquial Italian with an audio-visual course!

Flower Market

Via Trionfale (north of Vatican City)
Open Tuesdays only, 10 a.m. until 1 p.m.

4.7 Eating Out in Rome

Rome can be enjoyed sitting down. The locals spend much of their leisure at pavement cafés, gossiping and watching the world go by. Favourite drinks are tiny, extra-strong cups of Espresso coffee, or apéritifs like Campari soda.

There is infinite choice of café locations: in 16th-century piazzas, echoing with children at play; in side-streets, friendly as a village pub; at busy crossroads, providing ringside seats for the cut-and-thrust blood sport of Italian driving.

Along the Via Veneto, you can join Rome's café society. It's more expensive, but you are paying for the location, formerly the haunt of famous film stars.

Food? Just like everywhere else in Italy, there is good eating almost everywhere you go. Restaurants offer a Menu Turistico at fixed all-inclusive prices, and there are fast-food establishments of every type. But Rome has colourful restaurants by the thousand, and it's worth devoting part of your city break to the enjoyment of good food in surroundings that are loaded with atmosphere.

Try Some Roman Dishes

(. . . alla Romana), and the principal young local wines: Castelli Romani, Frascati and Colli Albani. The white Est-Est-Est is internationally known, coming from Montefiascone in the north of the Latium region. The red Cesanese from Olevano or Piglio is very palatable. A cool Trebbiano, from Aprilia in the area of ancient marshes drained centuries ago, is gaining a good reputation. Aleatico and Greghetto from Gradoli, and Sambuca from Viterbo are also excellent. If you are looking for a guarantee of origin and quality, ask for bottles with the DOC label (Denomination of Origin Controlled). They cost a bit more, but are worth it. In thirsty weather, Romans often mix the ordinary open wines with bubbly mineral water.

Abbacchio	– Roast baby lamb, cooked in white wine and with rosemary seasoning
Abbacchio alla cacciatora	– Lamb with an anchovy sauce
Broccoli romani	– Broccoli in white wine
Cannelloni	– Large pasta tubes, stuffed with various meat, and baked in cheese and tomato sauce
Carciofi alla giudia	– artichokes fried crisp in olive oil and lemon juice
Fettuccini	– Thin ribbon pasta made with a sauce of egg, butter, Parmesan cheese and anchovy
Piselli al prosciutto	– peas slowly cooked with Parma ham and diced bacon

Spaghetti all'amatriciana	– with a sauce of fresh tomatoes, bacon and the piquant Pecorino cheese
Spaghetti alla carbonara	– with garlic, peppers, bacon, cheese and egg
Saltimbocca	– slices of ham and veal, cooked together in butter and marsala sauce
Stracciatella	– clear soup with beaten egg and cheese
Suppli	– rice croquettes stuffed with Mozzarella cheese and minced meat

Restaurant Suggestions
Price guideline

Prices in the listed restaurants may be subject to change; and obviously everyone orders differently. But here's the price grading sytem:

£   = under £10, and frequently much less
££   = £10–£20
£££   = £20+

Trastevere Area

Cross the Tiber to the Trastevere district for colourful, typical restaurants that cheerfully cater for the tourist trade with perambulating musicians and flower-sellers. During the warmer months you dine outdoors, lingering over a 2-hour meal with a low-cost bottle or two of wine. On cooler evenings, service is indoors.

Sabatini   Piazza S. Maria in Trastevere 16   Tel: 582026
Famous for seafood. Also famous for prices! Good food, but among Rome's most expensive restaurants. Closed Wednesdays.   £££

La Tana de Noantri   Via della Paglia 1–3
Tel: 5896575
Near Piazza S. Maria. Very popular, excellent food and good value. Typical Roman dishes. Closed Tuesday.   ££

Ivo's Pizzeria   Via San Francesco Ripa   Tel: 5817082
Very crowded and lively. The best pizzas in Rome. Closed Tuesday.   £

Da Cenci   Via della Lungaretta 67   Tel: 582670
Excellent for seafood. Closed Sunday.   ££

Da Meo Pattaca   Piazza dei Mercanti   Tel: 5816198
Lively atmosphere with music and dancing.   ££

Arco di San Calisto   Via Arco di San Calisto
Tel: 6818323
Fish specialty. Closed Sunday.   ££

Via Veneto/Spanish Steps Area

Dal Bolognese   Piazza del Popolo   Tel: 361426
Opening in the evening from 20.30 onwards. Food expensive, but atmosphere excellent.   £££

Grotte Del Piccione   Via della Vite 37   Tel: 6795336
Friendly atmosphere. Pizza a speciality. Closed Monday.   £

Osteria Marcello   Via Aurora, near Via Veneto
Good Italian cooking, in lively surroundings.   £

Piccolo Mondo   Via Aurora 39   Tel: 4754595
For special occasions. Very expensive, but food and location make it worthwhile. Closed Sunday and August.   £££

Piazza Navona/Pantheon/Piazza Campo Dei Fiori

La Pollarolla   25 Piazza Pollarolla   Tel: 6541654
Roman specialities. Closed Monday.   £

La Carbonara   23 Piazza Campo dei Fiori
Tel: 6564783
Lovely setting on one of Rome's oldest squares. Closed Tuesday.   £

L'Orso 80   33 Via dell'Orso   Tel: 6564904
Try the antipasto. Closed Monday.   £

Vatican Area

La Fiorentina   Via Andrea Doria 22   Tel: 312310
Good food, but can be expensive. Specializes in pizzas cooked in a wood-fired oven. Friendly service, very popular. Closed Wednesday.   ££

Taverna Varrone   Via Varrone   Tel: 6530309
Closed Wednesday.   ££

Sardegna Inn   Via Candia 60   Tel: 386521
Sardinian specialities. Closed Monday.   ££

Taverna di Giovanni   Via del Banco di Santo Spirito
Tel: 6564116
Try their roast lamb speciality. Closed Monday.   ££

Termini Station Area

Est Est Est   Via Principe Amadeo   Tel: 4741319
Enjoy your meal with guitarist accompaniment. Closed Tuesday.   ££

La Mangrovia   Via Milazzo 6A   Tel: 4952754
Seafood in relaxing surroundings. Closed Sunday.   ££

Hostaria Fulvimari Via Principe Amedeo
Good Roman specialities; excellent pasta. Closed
Sunday.   £

Osteria de Benedetto Via Vicenza
Good food at reasonable prices. Closed Sunday.   £

Cafés and Bars

Can be divided into three categories: luxurious; typical average; and adequate. Most come in the middle category – welcome ports-of-call for visitors who want to relax from sightseeing, make a phone call, have a snack, go to the lavatory, or even have a cup of coffee. You'll find them everywhere!

The luxurious grade can be found especially in the Via Veneto, where you pay to be seen in one of the salubrious bars.

Café de Paris/Donays/Carpano
All in the Via Veneto
These three are definitely the salubrious type.

Antico Café Greco
Via Condotti (near Spanish Steps)
A place where you can join the smart set for afternoon aperitifs. Not to be missed by literary buffs, as it used to be the haunt of Mark Twain, Oscar Wilde and Hans Christian Andersen.

Tea Rooms
Babington's Tea Room
(foot of Spanish Steps)
This is just the place to recover after window shopping in the elegant streets nearby. Here you can enjoy muffins, pastries and proper pots of tea in an old-time English atmosphere.

Ice-Cream Parlours

You cannot visit Rome without treating yourself to an Italian ice-cream. From preference, go to a gelateria (ice-cream parlour), as their product is of much better quality than what is sold by street vendors.

Giolitti
Via Uffici del Vicario 40 (near Piazza Colonna)
This revered ice-cream parlour is probably the most popular in Rome. It gets very busy, but the ice-cream makes it more than worthwhile.

Nota Blu
Salita dei Crescenzi 3 (near Pantheon)
What could be better than home-made ice-cream and a table on the pavement in full view of the magnificent Pantheon? Remember it's very expensive to sit outside, but you can linger if you want.

Tre Scalini
Piazza Navona 30
Renowned for its 'tartufo', which is a rich chocolate ice-cream with chocolate chips through it, and topped with whipped cream.

Nightlife in Rome

Rome nightlife is generally noisy, gregarious and a friendly affair, especially in the summer months. There is usually a wide variety of outdoor concerts, film shows, fairs and exhibitions. The best way to check night-time events is to buy a local daily – 'Il Messagero' for example. Or study the English-language publication 'This Week in Rome', available at news-stands.

Dining out is part of the nightlife. During the warmer months, go to Trastevere – 'across the Tiber'. Wandering around and choosing an outdoor restaurant is part of the local scene, with musicians entertaining from table to table, and flower-sellers adding to the colour. Especially it is festive season in the second half of July, when wine flows extra freely and everyone's having fun.

Another evening, relax with a drink at a characteristic locality like the Piazza Navona, which has all the bubbly atmosphere of a film set.

By night, the ruins, monuments and fountains of Rome take on a more theatrical appearance, thanks to imaginative use of floodlights. It's worth going completely tourist, hiring a horse-carriage for an hour (agreeing the price first!), to go jogging around the floodlit city in the cooler evening. If you haven't already thrown your coin into the Trevi Fountain, make that essential pilgrimage after dark. Night-time, the lit-up monument stands out even more dramatically than by day. It's amusing to watch the coming and going of visitors, the arrival of the sightseeing coaches and the carriages, and the total blocking of the narrow streets around.

Nobody minds the traffic dislocation. Time is unimportant. You can extend your stay in pleasant local bars, absorbing the atmosphere through the open doorways.

Another amusement is the after-dinner stroll along Via Veneto, the haunt of 'café society', sitting at outdoor tables that line the pavements. From season to season, one café loses favour while another climbs, whenever the trendsetters of Rome switch allegiance.

How about a night at the opera? The Teatro dell'Opera is in full song from December to June, and the company then migrates to the deeply impressive setting of the Caracalla Baths for an open-air season, July to mid-August.

This gigantic Roman ruin, looming against the stars, makes a spectacular backdrop to the great scenes of Italian opera. Top favourite for Romans and tourists alike is Aïda. The seats are hard, so take padding. The evening air cools dramatically, so be prepared with a woolly. Intermissions are lengthy, and performances continue till past midnight. Have an afternoon siesta, and you won't doze off partway through. Special buses are available for returning to hotel districts.

Tickets for either the Opera House or the Baths are available at the Opera Box Office at Piazza Beniamino Gigli, 10-13 hrs. and 17-19 hrs.

Among the other regular musical events are concerts in the Basilica of Maxentius (June–August); winter season concerts of the Accademia Nazionale of Santa Cecilia; and winter concerts of the Accademia Filarmònico Romana.

Jazz Clubs

Musica Inn
Lungotevere dei Fiorentini
Tel: 6544934

Centro Jazz St Louis
Via del Cardello 13a
Tel: 483424

Mississippi Jazz Club
Borgo Angelico 16

Nightclubs

Be careful before entering nightclubs, as some are extremely expensive.

Acropolis
Via Luciani 52
Tel: 870504

Histeria
Via Giovannelli 12
Tel: 864587

Discos

Supersonic
Via Ovidio 17

Wednesdays and weekends. Good light show and loud music, usually New Wave.

Falcon Club
Via degli Avignonese
Favourite hangout for students, au pairs and a sprinkling of journalists.

4.9 Sunday in Rome

Excursions
A variety of excursions are available in Rome on a Sunday, so check once in Rome for details.

Markets
Porta Portese Market is open 7.00-13.00 hrs (beware of pickpockets).

Museums and Galleries
Many museums and galleries are open on Sundays (see earlier chapters for details).

Church Services

St Peter's, Vatican City
Services (hrs.)
09.00 High Altar
10.30 High Altar
11.00 San Guiseppe Altar
11.30 Capella del Sacramento
12.15 High Altar
13.00 San Guiseppe Altar
16.00 High Altar
17.00 Altar Vespers
17.30 High Altar

Papal Blessing is at 11.00 hrs at St Peter's in winter or at Castel Gondolfo in summer months.

St Paul's Within the Walls
Via Nazionale   Anglican Mass 8.30, 10.30 hrs.

4.10 At Your Service in Rome

Banks & Exchange Bureaux
Bank opening hours: Monday-Friday 8.30-13.30 hrs. Some banks re-open 14.45-15.45 hrs.

Exchange Bureaux (Cambio)
At Termini Station
Open: 8.30-21.00 hrs. (but may vary in winter). Other exchange bureaux open 9-13 hrs. and 15.30-19.30 hrs. Some close Saturdays.

Post Office & Telephone
General opening hours are 8.30-14.00 hrs; Saturday 8.30-12.00.

Main Post Office
Piazza Silvestro (near corner of Via del Corso and Via del Tritone)
Open: Monday-Friday 8.30-20.00 hrs; Saturday 8.30-18.00 hrs. Closed Sunday and Holy days.

It's best to make long-distance calls from a post office, as you can call direct and pay the normal charge. The Post Office in Piazza Silvestro has a telephone section – called the ASST office – right next door, open 8 a.m. till midnight.

Local Rome phone numbers can be weird, anything from four to eight digits long. Thus, the Vatican switchboard number is 6982. Just think of whisky, VAT 69, to get you started.

Dialling code for Rome from UK – 010-39-6; from USA or Canada – 011-39-6.

Emergency Phones
Police or Fire Brigade	113
Medical Assistance	338 3730
First Aid, Ambulance	5100

Useful Telephone Numbers and Addresses
Police Headquarters – Questura at Via Genova 2
Metro: Repubblica   Tel: 4686
English speakers are available 24 hours.

This police station never closes. Should you have anything stolen, you must report it to the police for insurance purposes, obtaining an official declaration of theft. If you're insured through your tour operator, report the loss also to the local representative.

If your passport is stolen, once you have the police report you should go to the British Consulate (adjoining the British Embassy) taking two passport size photographs. The Consulate will issue a temporary passport costing approximately 20,000 lire.

Lost Property
To claim any objects handed in to the Lost Property office, you must have a copy of the declaration made to the police. Phone enquiries are usually a waste of breath.

Municipal Lost Property Office
Via Nicola Bettoni 1 (in Trastevere district, a few blocks north of Testaccio Bridge)   Tel: 581604
Open: Monday-Saturday 9-12 hrs.

ATAC – For Losses on City Transport
Via Volturno 65 (near Termini Station).

Embassies

British – Via XX Settembre 80A
Tel: 475 5441; 475 5551
American – Via Veneto 119A Tel: 4674
Canadian – Via Zara 30 Tel: 844 1841/5
Australian – Via Alessandria 215 Tel: 841241
Irish – Largo Nazareno 3 Tel: 678 2541

Recommended Reading

A bewildering number of books cover virtually every possible viewpoint and special interest. Try these two: Georgina Masson – *A Companion Guide to Rome* – Collins H. V. Morton – *A Traveller in Rome* – Methuen: An old edition but very readable, explaining the history of Rome around its monuments.

Further Information

If you require any further holiday information before you travel, contact the Italian State Tourist Office (E.N.I.T. for short):

GREAT BRITAIN – 1 Princes Street, London W1R 8AY. Tel: (01) 408-1254.
USA EAST COAST – 630 Fifth Avenue, Suite 1565, New York, NY 10111. Tel: (212) 245-4822/4.
USA MID WEST – 500 North Michigan Avenue, Chicago, IL 60611. Tel: (312) 644 0990/1.
USA WEST COAST – 360 Post Street, Suite 801, San Francisco, CA 94109. Tel: (415) 392 6206/7.
CANADA – Store 56, Plaza 3, Place Ville-Marie, Montreal, Quebec. Tel: (514) 866 7667.
AUSTRALIA – c/o Alitalia, AGC House, 124 Philip St., Sydney, NSW 2000. Tel: (2) 22-13-620.
NEW ZEALAND – c/o Alitalia, 95 Queen St., Auckland. Tel: (9) 79-44-55.
SOUTH AFRICA – London House, 21 Loveday Street, Johannesburg 2000 (P.O. Box 6507). Tel: 83-83-247.